HOPE

David Chandler's *Hope* offers a compelling exploration of the politics of hope against the backdrop of a broken world grappling with global crises, from political disillusionment to catastrophic climate change, where alternative futures seem difficult to imagine in positive terms.

Examining hope as an ethicopolitical praxis, Chandler offers a highly readable analysis of how hope can sustain alternative futures amidst widespread uncertainty and disillusionment, critically engaging with hope's transformative potential, and challenging conventional political approaches and envisioning new ways of thinking about trust, care and relational politics. It traces the concept of hope through diverse critical traditions, including the Frankfurt School, Black Radical Tradition, Queer Utopianism, Critical Indigenous Studies and contemporary Critical Black Studies, and delves into the social and historical contexts of hope, analysing its role in communities of survivance, struggle and experimentation. Crucially, and uniquely, the author emphasises the human subject's centrality to hope, exploring how unconscious desires and liberated imaginations can foster new political imaginaries and connecting theoretical insights with practical applications for navigating today's critical challenges.

A thought-provoking examination of how struggles to keep futural possibilities alive in the present strive to move beyond a politics that can only reproduce more of the same, *Hope* is essential reading for students and scholars of environmental humanities, politics and the social sciences.

David Chandler is Professor of International Relations, University of Westminster, London, UK. He edits the journal *Anthropocenes - Human, Inhuman, Posthuman* and writes widely on the subjects of critical theory, the contemporary crisis of governance and race in the Anthropocene.

'Chandler's *Hope* is a tour de force in its mapping of contemporary political and social theory. It is an important provocation that carves out lines of hope beyond the world as it exists. Without these, there can only be the violent solace of hope as a feeling, rather than hope as a strategy. This book is essential reading for anyone working in theory today.'

Claire Colebrook, *Professor of English Literature, Monash University*

'This concise book offers a much-needed, critical intervention into the ways a whole range of political, community and scholarly projects "utilis[e] hope as a remaining resource in the wake of broken worlds". Chandler brings our attention to under-examined critical "engagements with hope", including those emerging from continental philosophical traditions, black studies, and decolonial approaches, which strive "to hold open the future' and imagine worlds otherwise."

Louiza Odysseos, *Professor Emeritus in International Relations in the School of Global Studies, University of Sussex*

'David Chandler carefully examines the ontologies and meanings of hope. He analyses how hope today has been instrumentalised, often limiting rather than enabling the emergence of alternative futures. Kant's question, "What may I hope for?" still remains a crucial concern, especially when thinking beyond survivance.'

Elena Korosteleva, *Professor of Politics and Global Sustainable Development, University of Warwick*

‘This book offers a timely reconsideration of hope, at a time when it seems both more necessary and more difficult than ever. Much more than hoping for rosy futures, the challenging ideas woven through this book are meant to disrupt modernist and normative notions of hope, and bring the discussion about hope to the core problem of its ambiguous ontology.’

Noga Glucksam, *author of* Rewilding Peace,
Department of Political Science,
University College London

Shortcuts
Little Books on Big Issues

Series editor:
Anthony Elliott, Adelaide University, Australia

ABOUT THE BOOK SERIES:

Shortcuts is a major new series of concise, accessible introductions to some of the key global issues of our times. The series is developed as an A to Z coverage of emergent or novel social, cultural and political developments. Issues and topics covered range from food to fat, from climate change to suicide bombing, from hope to social futures. Whilst the principal focus of *Shortcuts* is the relevance of current issues to the social sciences and humanities, the books will also appeal to a wider audience seeking guidance on how to engage with today's leading social, political and philosophical debates. Short and concise, the books will provide cutting-edge insights into the pressing realities of our lives in these times.

Anthony Elliott is Distinguished Professor of Sociology at Adelaide University, where he is Executive Director of the Jean Monnet Centre of Excellence for Digital Transformations. He is Super-Global Visiting Professor at Keio University, Japan and Visiting Professor at University College Dublin, Ireland.

ALSO IN THE SERIES:

FREEDOM, 2ND EDITION

Nick Stevenson

Hope
David Chandler

Living Futures
Deborah Lupton

Anti-Science
Dariusz Jemielniak

Food
John Coveney

Zombies
Jennifer Rutherford

Love
Tom Inglis

Panic
Keith Tester

Planet Sport
Kath Woodward

Global Finance
Robert Holton

Freedom
Nick Stevenson

Web 2.0
Sam Han

Suicide Bombings
Riaz Hassan

Feelings
Stephen Frosh

Confronting Climate Change
Constance Lever-Tracy

For more information about this series, please visit: https://www.routledge.com/Shortcuts/book-series/SCUTS

HOPE

SHORTCUTS TO A BIG IDEA

David Chandler

Routledge
Taylor & Francis Group
LONDON AND NEW YORK

Designed cover image: Getty Images

First published 2027
by Routledge
4 Park Square, Milton Park, Abingdon, Oxon OX14 4RN

and by Routledge
605 Third Avenue, New York, NY 10158

Routledge is an imprint of the Taylor & Francis Group, an informa business

British Library Cataloguing-in-Publication Data
A catalogue record for this book is available from the British Library

ISBN: 9781041058687 (hbk)
ISBN: 9781041058656 (pbk)
ISBN: 9781003632719 (ebk)

DOI: 10.4324/9781003632719

Typeset in Sabon
by KnowledgeWorks Global Ltd.

CONTENTS

ACKNOWLEDGEMENTS

This book has been on my to-do list for over a decade. In 2013, my book *Freedom vs Necessity in International Relations: Human-Centred Approaches to Security and Development* was published; I had wanted the title to be much more along the Nietzschean lines of 'Human, All Too Human' but the publishers disagreed. Worse, I was not really satisfied with my ability to get to grips with the human-centred problematic, then taking over the policy-making world, and wanted to more fully engage the left or critical orientation at the heart of these approaches. This was the basis for wishing to engage more with hope as a critical discourse centring human agency, vulnerability, adaptation and resilience. I guess this is a roundabout way of saying that given the gestation period of this book there are a lot of people to thank, too many, so I will keep my acknowledgements brief.

Over the period of working on this book, I have been one of the organisers of the Materialisms Reading Group, meeting monthly at the University of Westminster, and in addition, over the last five years, an online network, the Black Anthropocene Working Group. I would like to thank the folks involved in these forums, particularly Jonathan Pugh, Farai Chipato, Harshavardhan Bhat, Marie Petersmann, Paul Rekret, Khalil Saucier, Tryon Woods, Matthew Gravlin, Chris Zebrowski, Caroline von Taysen, Stuart Watson, Zí Jiao, Ignasi Torrent, Rob Cowley and Allan Parsons.

I would also like to thank the organisers and audience members at events over the last year or so where some of the key themes of this book were discussed, in particular: the 'Underworlds – Sites and Struggles of Global Dis/Ordering' conference, London School of Economics/ Queen Mary University of London, May 2024; the 'Working with the Negative' European Workshops in International Studies, Istanbul, July 2024; the 'Hopeful Attachments on a Ruined Planet' conference, Hamburg, October 2024; the Security and Resilience seminar, Coventry University, February 2025; the *Race in the Anthropocene* workshop, London, February 2025; the International Studies Association annual convention, Chicago, March 2025; the Research in Progress seminar, University of Westminster, April 2025; the 'Securing Resilient Futures' conference, University of Nottingham Ningbo, May 2025; the Polycritical Law workshop, London School of Economics, May 2025; the 'Refusal Centred Indigenous Research Ethics and Methodologies' panel, University of Cambridge, May 2025; the 'Weather Politics in the Caribbean' conference, University of the West Indies, Kingston, May 2025; the Dauphine Philosophical Workshop 'Negative Ontologies of Time', London, June 2025; the 'Planning and Publics - On Sustaining Shared Futurities in a Planetary Era' workshop, New York University, London, June 2025; and 'The Future of Social Sciences' symposium, University of Warwick, July 2025.

Also, special thanks to the small team of colleagues I have been writing on hope with over the last few years, Sebastian Schindler, Pol Bargues and Valerie Waldow and, most of all, to Paulina Tambakaki, without whom this book would not have been possible.

INTRODUCTION

The whole interest of my reason, whether speculative or practical, is concentrated in the three following questions: What can I know? What should I do? What may I hope?
Immanuel Kant, *Critique of Pure Reason*

INTRODUCTION

Hope is essential to a liberal imaginary, as the epigraph above, a much-quoted line from Kant, makes clear. Hope is inextricable from understandings of the world and the human. For many writers and policymakers today, especially when it comes to politics, hope is in short supply. In a time where it is easier to imagine the end of the world than it is to imagine the end of capitalism,[1] it seems that politics can provide few answers to the problems that are faced in this broken world. In these circumstances, it is easy to think that the capacity for hope is exhausted. Philosopher Richard Rorty (1999, 230) argues that political hope has been lost 'in so far as there has been a loss of faith in cosmopolitan and universalist notions... [as] a result of the increasing inability to believe that things could ever get much better than they are now'. For Rorty, this age is one of lost hope and the hope that has been lost is the hope that was placed in politics, as a sphere through which change and social transformation were possible.

The problem at the heart of this loss, for Rorty, is societal 'inability to construct a plausible narrative of

DOI: 10.4324/9781003632719-1

progress' (1999, 232); the fact that there has been '[a] turn away from narration and utopian dreams toward philosophy seems to me a gesture of despair' (Rorty 1999). This loss of hope in progress has been called 'the slow cancellation of the future' by Franco 'Bifo' Beradi (2011, 18). The dissipation of hope can also be seen in the collection of essays edited by Peter Thompson and Slavoj Žižek, *The Privatization of Hope* (2013), in which the contributors argue that the collapse of organised political movements and the 'atomization of workers and their unfair one-sided submission to the needs of the market and capital isolate individual hope... [and] threatens to turn dreams and hopes into the lone activity of online-hermits' (Vidal and Schröter 2013, 297–298). For these theorists and thinkers, hope is held to be endangered and in need of careful attention as an emotion, a practice, a skill, a virtue even, that is more necessary today than perhaps ever before.

Radical philosophers, such as Rorty and Žižek, are, of course, correct that, viewed from a particular perspective, hope is exhausted. If hope is understood to be hope in a revolutionary or programmatic transformative political project with the state at its centre, then yes, hope appears to be in short supply. It is true that for a long time 'hope' has served merely as a shorthand for hope in progressive politics (Potkay 2024, 49), highlighted, of course, in US President Obama's (2008) 'Hope' poster and autobiography, *The Audacity of Hope* (2008). However, this hope, celebrated in demands to keep hope 'alive', for critical theorists, such as Lewis R. Gordon (2024, 155–156), is problematic: 'What is hope in that regard but a call for an alignment of the dispositions that maintain the social fabric of an oppressing society?'. Where this book could be said to disagree with Rorty, Žižek and Gordon is in their restriction of hope to hope in the liberal political imaginary (see also Žižek 2018, xiv; Warren 2015, 16–17).

The closures of catastrophic climate change and the Anthropocene as an age of human-induced environmental crisis have heightened the already existing critical tensions in approaches to and understandings of hope: Hope for what? Hope for who? Without a telos of progress, every concrete articulation of hope seems even more partial, even more limited, even more problematic in an interdependent and inter-related world. Every hope for inclusion then creates new modes of exclusion. Every attempt to resolve a problem then merely defers, displaces or disavows the actual problem (think building roads to overcome traffic congestion, building seawalls to cope with sea level rises, building more prisons to deal with social problems) imagining that society can continue as before. Every hope for something, no matter what it may be, involves at the same time a disavowal of its costs to others. Questions of white privilege haunt every aspiration of salvage or repair (see, for example, Puar 2017). No hope can be pure or innocent when the threatened closure of futurity pits livability for some against the loss of liveable lives of others. If hope is to have a future, then it cannot be a hope that is not cogniscent of the disastrousness of this world. It cannot be a naïve hope that makes claims to alternative futures without a consideration of privilege and positionality, without an awareness that the present cannot just be put to oneside, of the fact that 'the future is already here, it is just not evenly distributed'.[2]

Hope: Shortcuts to a Big Idea considers the possibilities for hope today. It will argue that taking seriously the impact of social and political closures, hope is increasingly drawn upon for alternative ethicopolitical praxes, distinguished from liberal political imaginaries, and working in ways that seek to challenge and go beyond these constraints. What dominant approaches miss, then, is engagements with hope which struggle to hold open the future and to see beyond the world as it appears. The hope that is the focus of this book is the sort of hope summoned by Ashon Crawley's *Blackpentecostal Breath* (2017), a 'resource that is plenteous, that exists in plenitude… the gift, the concept, the inhabitation of and living into *otherwise possibilities*... infinite alternatives to what *is*' (2017, 2 italics in original). Hope imagined in this way is utilised to hold open alternative futures in the face of disillusionment in formal political processes, in the face of the violence and exclusions which seem to be built into collective ways of life, and the closures of climate catastrophes and global warming which call an end to the liberal telos of progress. Hope so conceived enables a sensitivity towards something beyond what is, beyond the disastrous, catastrophic and genocidal appearances of *this* world. As Crawley states:

> ...what *is* is about being, about existence, about ontology. But if infinite alternatives exist, if otherwise possibility is a resource that is never exhausted what *is*, what exists, is but one of many. Otherwise possibilities exist alongside that which we can detect with our finite sensual capacities.
>
> (Crawley 2017, 2)

The question then is 'How to detect such... possibility otherwise, such alternative to what is as a means to disrupt the current configurations of power and inequity? How to detect, how to produce and inhabit otherwise epistemological fields' (2017, 2–3). The answer, for Crawley, lies in the belief of and in Black Study. For other theorists and advocates of hope the tasks lie in allied and analogous fields of work, often related to a critical tradition that insists that the world, as given in the liberal imaginary, has 'something missing'; that, through the radical work of freeing the senses or the imagination, another reality can be accessed beyond the reductionist, abstract, binary and divisive categories that construct this contemporary world of racial exclusion and climate catastrophe.

While there is a discussion about the loss of hope in *this* world and its institutions, beliefs and practices, another approach to hope is increasingly coming into view. This book argues that a belief in the possibility of otherwise worlds is increasingly central to how *this* world is understood and to understandings of political possibility (King et al 2020). This approach to hope is not focused upon traditional state-based projects, parties and programmes but sees hope as essential for informing a struggle for open and uncertain futures in the face of multiple closures of possibility. Rather than hope being privatised and pushed to the margins of politics, politics itself appears to be being transformed. Political action and practices are increasingly held to be taking place in the world itself, no longer mediated through the sphere of formal and bureaucratic political parties and institutions. Hope as an ethicopolitical approach is thereby less likely to consider the role and importance of states or to understand governance as a process of 'top-down' direction and management.

Hope is being drawn upon for imaginaries of futural possibility in ways that attempt to respond precisely to the problems outlined by Rorty, Žižek and Lewis. The desire to problematise the frameworks of understanding of the liberal political order and to challenge the privatised and atomised liberal subject is at the heart of hope's utilisation for alternative ethicopolitical approaches, articulated through (anti)political struggles for new 'genres' of the human (Wynter 2003), or for 'reenchanting the human' (Wynter and Scott 2000). The fragmentation of the political realm and loss of legitimacy of governing institutions, alongside the uncertainties and disruptions of a broken world seemingly in permanent crisis, mean that hope is more central to life than ever before.

In these times of polycrisis, complexity, interdependence and entanglements, this is unlikely to be hope in a project or an idea that exists 'out there' in some sort of pure form. In a world of uncertainty, hope is no longer in reference to discrete actions, or relations, understood as ways of working to achieve certain positive outcomes held to be uncertain but possible. Hope increasingly becomes enrolled in discussions of behavioural attitudes or dispositions, of modes of being in the world, modes that are not necessarily calculated and goal-directed but rather processual and open-ended.

This introductory chapter introduces the concept of hope itself in three main sections. The first section briefly introduces hope as an increasingly ubiquitous concept and provides a brief history of hope, including an analysis of how hope has been traditionally distinguished from optimism and from utopianism. The second section focuses on how hope is engaged with today in instrumentalised ways, in policy discourses and in academia, particularly in the fields of analytical philosophy and social psychology. The third section considers how hope has been utilised differently, within ethicopolitical undertakings, rather than merely as the adjunct to existing understandings of politics as a sphere of activity. The final section provides an overview of the chapters of the book.

WHAT IS HOPE?

Hope is a concept with a long history, during which time its meaning and usage has often been ambiguous and regularly contested. Ambiguity is at the centre of hope as a term that necessarily problematises binaries, working on the edge of divisions between the present and the future, science and speculation, reason and unreason, even of ontology and epistemology (Thompson 2013, 84). The ambiguity of hope can already be seen in the opening section of this chapter, where hope was, on the one hand, a belief in something (the modernist political project), and, on the other hand, described as a practice or way of relating to the world. In fact, the question whether hope is a state of mind – a mental, emotional, affective state – or a practice – that is, a life skill, even a capacity 'multiplier', highlights some of the issues at stake in hope's deployment in struggles to hold open alternative futures (van der Lugt 2025, 86).

The history of hope is mostly one that is critical of the concept. Hope was widely criticised in classical antiquity and onwards through the Renaissance and into the Enlightenment as an illusion or a distraction from the need to focus on the present moment (Potkay 2024, 49). If one hoped it was a sign of vanity or presumption, a challenge to the gods, and a potentially self-destructive attraction to impossible or unachievable goals. Hope was a product of vanity or ignorance, preventing a serious engagement with the reality of the world. For the ancient Greeks, destiny lay in the hands of the gods, so hope was not rational. Despite this 'bigger metaphysical perspective', hope still existed as a concept, if an ambiguous one (Gulliford 2024, 211).

Famously, Hesiod wrote of hope in his story of Pandora, created by Zeus as a punishment for Prometheus's theft of fire. She is told not to open a jar, but stirred by curiosity, she does, and all the evils fly out, but as she closes it, one remains, 'hope' (*elpis*) (Snow 2024b, 2). There has been no shortage of discussion as to the meaning of this, whether hope is therefore an evil or, in fact, a good, an antidote to evil. For Friedrich Nietzsche, this last evil was left in Pandora's jar by Zeus, not as a blessing but as a punishment (van der Lugt 2025, 79). Nietzsche argued that although man mistakenly 'takes the remaining evil for the greatest worldly good', Zeus wanted man to have hope so that he would not:

> ...throw his life away no matter how much the other evils might torment him, but rather to go on letting himself be tormented anew. To that end, he gives man hope. It is in truth the most evil of all evils because it prolongs man's torment.
>
> (Nietzsche 2004, 58)

It is with Christianity that hope first comes to the fore as a positive virtue, and it is often argued that hope's history is deeply inflected by Christian theology (van der Lugt 2025, 26). Here, its value comes precisely in its opposition to despair, then (as now) the unforgivable sin.

Medieval philosopher and Roman Catholic saint Thomas Aquinas argued that hope was intermediate between two extremes which were sins or vices, presumption and despair; hope was a striving uncertain of attaining its goals, rather than certain of success or failure (Snow 2024b, 2, 5). Aquinas was central in articulating hope's agential capacity, asserting that while faith may be hope's precondition, it was only hope that enabled the subject to work for the eternal grace that can never be guaranteed (Swenson-Lengyel 2024, 164).

The need to live with uncertainty and doubt is therefore an essential characteristic of hope as a practice. In fact, according to the Bible, hope is central to the moral life of a religious community, on the basis that where there is faith, there is always hope (Potkay 2024, 55). As St. Paul famously stated in 1 Corinthians 13: 12–13:

> For now we see through a glass, darkly; but then [at the end of time, in an afterlife] face to face: now I know in part; but then shall I know even as also I am known. And now abideth faith, hope, charity, these three; but the greatest of these is charity.
>
> (Potkay 2024, 55)

Charity (love) remains while faith and hope are no longer necessary in the afterlife. Hope, of course, is required in the present, always the time of struggle and suffering, coping and resilience.

In modernity, with the secularised telos of the Enlightenment project, hope becomes a background assumption of progress rather than a question of suffering, struggle or persistence. In fact, as Terry Eagleton argues, hope is literally baked into a modern ontology by Immanuel Kant, for whom nature, 'Providence' itself, ensures that human practice, though operating blindly, leads to human betterment: 'Hope, so to speak, is built into the structure of reality itself' (Eagleton 2017, 8). In this way, Kant shifted the contemporary understanding of hope from being a passion or emotional state to a cognitive state essential to acting rationally in the world.

Kant secularised and racialised hope, as will be considered later in this book. Hope was secularised in that the appearances of the world were never all that there was. In fact, the reality of the world was always impossible to access. This is the cut between the phenomenon as experienced and the noumena which is inaccessible. So, for Kant, otherwise worlds were always possible and existing in the here and now beyond perception. Without this, we would be stuck only with a limited 'reality'. Kant's 1795 (1970) essay 'Perpetual Peace' makes exactly this claim for otherwise worlds articulated in opposition to and in reparation for the disastrousness of *this* one:

> … the *inhospitable* conduct of the civilized states of our continent, especially the commercial states, the injustice which they display in *visiting* foreign countries and peoples (which in their case is the same as *conquering* them) seems appallingly great. America, the negro countries, the Spice Islands, the Cape, etc. were looked upon at the time of their discovery as ownerless territories, for the native inhabitants counted the inhabitants as nothing. In East India (Hindustan), foreign troops were brought in under the pretext of merely setting up trading posts. This led to oppression of the natives, incitement of the various Indian states to widespread wars, famine, insurrection, treachery, and the whole litany of evils which can afflict the human race. (Kant 1970, 106)

It was the disastrousness of this world, its 'whole litany of evils', that necessitated hope as a mode of acting otherwise, 'as if' another world was possible (see also Chandler 2025). However, for hope to guide practice, it was necessary that minds could be freed from the immediacy of appearances. It was this binary between the self-determining subject and people bound to and determined by their immediate surroundings (Silva 2007), that constituted the gap between those on 'the deck' and those in 'the hold' (Ferdinand 2022).

This book is a study of contemporary approaches to hope, increasingly articulated via alternative ethicopolitical imaginaries, which seek to hold the future open and the space for otherwise possibilities. Today, hope is increasingly central for a range of political and ethical discourses. These range from what to do when confronted with the apparent closures of the Anthropocene and catastrophic global warming, when technological and scientific solutions appear to be part of the problem, to questions of marginalisation, oppression and exclusion which appear to be reproduced regardless of the political system or location in the world. Hope is drawn upon to enable openings towards other ways of being, ones that evade or work otherwise to dominant imaginaries, problematising fixed understandings of entities and subjectivities. For these reasons, it is important to distinguish these political and analytical utilisations of hope from the everyday use of the word 'hope' in reference to positive, wishful or fanciful thinking (Cuervo and Cook 2019).

To begin to analyse the key characteristics of hope, it is important to clarify how hope is often considered to be conceptually distinct from optimism and utopianism (these considerations will be important in later chapters of the book). Hope is held to occupy a liminal position when it comes to political thought and conceptualisation, enrolled into ethicopolitical alternatives to that which exists, but at the same time aware of two pitfalls. These pitfalls are, firstly, the dangers of reproducing the exclusions and hierarchies of the present; this is the problem of optimism. And, secondly, of disavowal, the danger of seeking naïvely to imagine that there is any easy escape or 'beyond' to this world, as if the future were some pure open space rather than one already impacted upon by the oppressions and exclusions of the past and the present; this is the problem of utopianism.

Optimism can be understood to be a positive mindset, an approach that seeks to accentuate the positive, the possibilities that are present in the situation. Optimism and hope are often confused or conflated. However, hope seeks to provide an alternative ethicopolitical imaginary, opening up possibilities for rethinking categories of understanding, problematising long-standing assumptions of political agency, where it is located and how it might operate. This is very different to discussions of the politics involved in optimism. In contrast to hope, optimism restricts imaginaries to the kinds of problems and solutions that already exist and have provided the context within which the problem has arisen in the first place. Thus, hope tends to be linked to practices of struggle, of resistance, refusal and survivance rather than with accepting the terms which exist and merely being concerned with specific problems and specific ends.

Optimism (in relation to discussions of politics) is seen, therefore, as a double-edged sword: in some cases, being optimistic is vital for struggles for survival against terrible odds, essential for continuing, for experimenting in new ways and for being resilient against the crushing power of oppressive authorities. In other contexts, being optimistic can be problematic, leading to the acceptance of minor reforms or to being patient and subdued in the face of bureaucratic authority and the denial of rights. There are many studies of the politics of hope, which thus conflate hope with optimism. These studies often focus on the struggles of subaltern or marginalised groups who are often dependent on the goodwill or largess of hegemonic authorities.

In cases of asylum rights (Herz et al 2022; Kallio et al 2021), migrant issues (Fontanari 2019) or Indigenous rights (Lindroth and Sinevaara-Niskanen 2022), for example, commentators often make the point that the hope for a better life, that dependent and marginalised communities often manifest, is used against them by authorities, who governmentalise hope as a mechanism for compliance and subordination (see also, Gäckle 2024). In such cases, 'hopelessness' is enabling, as no longer believing in the possibilities of solutions within the present contextualisation of the problem can provide the courage to think in new and creative ways (Žižek 2018). Confusing optimism and hope can then lead to semantic disagreements where some commentators support hope as enabling ways beyond the world as it exists while others argue that hopelessness is enabling in these ways (for example, Cuervo and Cook 2019).

Hope also needs to be distinguished from utopianism. Sometimes utopianism is used in ways that closely parallel that of hope as articulated here. Both hope and utopianism challenge an acceptance of the world as it appears for hegemonic modes of thought and seek to move beyond linear temporalities, which are seen to disavow agential possibilities and creative potentials. However, utopianism tends to place its emphasis on futural imaginaries with little attention to events of the past or the relations and struggles of the present. In utopian futural imaginaries, there is often a complete ontological break, whereas for hope, as it is articulated in this book, there is always hope *in* the present itself. For writers concerned with hope, the past is often an important resource to be mobilised and to be repurposed and attention is given to the difficult question of how to ground futural imaginaries in the potentialities of the here and now. The ethico-political imaginaries of hope would not countenance acts that refuse any political future, such as Ghassan Hage's analysis of the politics of 'stuckedness' (2009), any more than they could accept a politics that makes a complete break from the past.

One example of the conflation of hope and utopianism is that of work that follows Jonathan Lear (2008) in framing 'radical hope' as a complete ontological and temporal break (see, for example, Kallio et al 2021). Lear's *Radical Hope* (2008) describes the Crow Chief Plenty Coups' radical imagination of starting again after the ontological loss occasioned by colonial devastation; the Crow's loss of their traditional modes of existence and resettlement on a government reservation (2008). It is therefore important to distinguish the ethicopolitical engagements with hope presented here from radical assertions of a break with the past that tend towards apologia and disavowal. Such a break is imagined in the statement by the Director of the University of Oxford's Pitt Rivers Museum, that 'radical hope' might enable the museum to escape its 'deep roots in coloniality' (Van Broekhoven 2020) through a future that symbolises a complete reimagining of the institution. Whereas utopianism ontologically cuts the future from the past, hope is utilised in ethicopolitical approaches which seek to work with 'reality' differently, to highlight the presence of alternative futures in the present. Hope is about holding the future open precisely through grasping a reality that is available beyond the limits and constraints of hegemonic structures of thought (Waldow et al 2024; Chandler 2024a).

HOPE TODAY

It's important to underline that contemporary approaches to hope, utilised for concerns with futurity and with keeping future possibilities alive in the present, have received relatively little academic investigation. Hope has been traditionally dealt with largely in the fields of theology, in philosophy, particularly in the field of analytical philosophy, and in applied and social psychology, rather than being considered as a political or ethicopolitical problematic. In these dominant framings, the meaning of hope itself is broadly taken as given, in line with an individual desire for a future object which is considered good but is not taken for granted. The questions then revolve around the need to encourage or nurture hope as a skill or capacity.

In this way, the contemporary academic and policy-related discussion of hope tends to focus upon affective-cognitive understandings and the domain of behaviour and behaviour-modification, emphasising individual agency and choice and the contexts through which this might be affected (Webb 2024, 293). This mode of discussing and instrumentalising hope is very much determined by a desire to maintain and improve the existing order of things. Hope is the one thing that cannot be lost in both Christian and modern philosophical accounts of the necessity of struggle and suffering. For this reason, hope has been effectively turned into a discipline in both senses of the word. This 'disciplinary' use of hope is chiefly articulated in two frameworks, those of analytical philosophy and of social psychology.

Hope has become increasingly important in the field of analytical philosophy since the publication of analytical philosopher John Patrick Day's article 'Hope' in the *American Philosophical Quarterly* in 1969. Day established what is called the 'standard' or 'orthodox' model of hope that: '"A hopes that P" is true if and only if "A wishes that P, and A thinks that P has some degree of probability, however small" is true' (cited in Snow 2024b, 8). This 'standard account' builds on Hobbes's definition of hope: 'Appetite with an opinion of attaining is called HOPE' and that of Aquinas: 'Hope is a movement of appetite aroused by the perception of what is agreeable, future, arduous, and possible of attainment' (cited in Chignell 2024, 134 n.2). For analytical philosophy then, hope is not an emotion, but a desire plus a probability-estimate. This 'standard' account often forms the basis for discussion and disagreement over whether this account is sufficient or is lacking in some way.

For example, Philip Pettit develops the distinction between 'superficial hope' which does not take much effort and 'substantial hope' which comes into play in times of desperation, enabling the maintenance of focus and goals (Snow 2024b, 11). Pettit focuses on the importance of 'cognitive resolve' that enables hope against the appearances of the limited chances of success; a similar approach to 'resolute hope' is forwarded by Adrienne Martin (see discussion in Webb 2024, 291–292). Andrew Chignell has also challenged the 'standard theory', suggesting that hope requires more than a 'barebones' analytic of desire (the conative element) plus a belief that an outcome is possible (the cognitive element), arguing that the key to hope is dispositional (2024, 110). By dispositional, Chignell seeks to emphasise the importance of the subject's focus on achieving the desired outcome.

This instrumental treatment of hope is also prevalent in the other major field through which hope is discussed today, social psychology, and in particular the field of positive psychology (Gulliford 2024). Definitions of hope here are rooted in cognitive learning theories and typically rely on the inter-relation between the expectancy of an event occurring and the actions taken to realise it (Oettingen 2024, 255). According to the late Charles Snyder, the concept of hope consists of two factors: 'agency thinking'; and 'pathways thinking'. Agency thinking describes the belief in the ability to achieve one's goals, and pathways describes the routes towards these – together these form the 'will and the ways' of hope (Snyder cited by Gulliford 2024, 208). Focus on the 'will' of hope leads to the psychological emphasis on individual self-esteem or self-confidence so that the work of hoping can continue under trying circumstances. Rather than being an intangible attribute, Snyder's reduction of hope to these two elements, available as measurable variables, has enabled hope to enter the world of policymaking and problem-solving through the ability to 'measure an individual's capacity for hope' (Edwards and McConnell 2024, 229).

Hope theory in psychological discourses is of practical benefit to individuals who are seeking to translate desired goals into strategies for achieving them. In this context, there is a link between hope and optimism, as 'positive' approaches enable individuals to take a step back from immediate experiences and patterns of behaviour to focus on opportunities for progress. Yet, this hope needs to be carefully managed (Gulliford 2024, 222). Gabriele Oettingen, for example, writes about how hope can be trained through mental contrasting: 'juxtaposing one's dreams and future fantasies with the obstacles of reality... helps to set priorities as people now pursue feasible futures but refrain from wasting their time and efforts on futures that can never be reached' (2024, 265). For others, hope is a disposition towards the world and as such can be understood as a mode of being that can be cultivated, practiced and worked upon in order to live well and to gradually perfect a way of being that neither falls into overconfidence nor gives way to despair (Han-Pile and Stern 2024).

As a disposition towards the world, hoping well involves practical work upon the self, honing productive modes of relationality that enable the world to be engaged with through 'a set of skills and abilities developed through years of engagement with self and world, and through previous instances of hoping' (Han-Pile and Stern 2024, 97). This mode of hoping, understood as developing an optimal mode of relational sensitivity, neither too active nor too passive (Han-Pile and Stern 2024, 98), needs to be taught from childhood, almost as an aesthetic sensitivity. In this way, hoping well enables the management of a world of uncertainty, through the 'psychology of aspirational control':

> ... agents must develop, and act in the light of, a keen awareness of their dependence on, and vulnerability to, circumstances beyond their control... Those who hope, or seek to cultivate hope, do not understand themselves as self-assured, autonomous agents but as relatively fragile selves, who exercise their agency medio-passively, in the full awareness that their success (if any) will depend at least as much on the cooperation of the world as on themselves.
>
> (Han-Pile and Stern 2024, 98)

Hope thus becomes a necessary but also a difficult attribute, requiring significant epistemic and ethical skills. For Edwards and McConnell, hope has a great deal of explanatory value for differential outcomes and is 'associated with increased academic and athletic performance and various indicators of well-being', while longitudinal studies have demonstrated 'that hope actually promotes resilience in adults over time' (2024, 229). For American environmentalist Wendell Berry, hope was the product of work, something to be cultivated as a practical art 'not merely a competent knowledge of... facts and processes, but also a complex set of attitudes, a certain culturally evolved stance' (cited in Lamb 2024, 354). Once hope becomes instrumentalised as a skill or a learned disposition, social psychology operates as a field that then begins to socially differentiate populations on the basis of these abilities. The capacity or capability to hope then becomes explanatory of social, economic and political differentials, influenced by culture and upbringing (see the discussion of 'resilience' in Chapter 3).

As the instrumental and policy-related fields of analytical hope and psychological hope continue to expand there seems to be an infinite variety of prefixes which include 'fearful hope', 'basal hope', 'psychological hope', 'open-ended hope', 'goal-directed hope', 'pessimistic hope', 'anxious hope', 'radical hope', 'pathological hope', 'sound hope', 'patient hope', 'critical hope', 'resolute hope', 'complex hope', 'robust hope', 'desiderative hope', 'epistemic hope' and 'transformative hope' among many others (see, for example, Snow 2024a). Sometimes hope is narrowly focused on being goal-directed, at other times hope theorists insist that hope should be more a way of being in the world, a disposition that enables individuals to enhance their agency in more flexible or fluid ways, as 'the outcome of human action is always indeterminate' (Webb 2024, 283).

Today, as noted above, the loss of hope in modernity's promises of social progress and liberal democratic futures frames the utilisation of hope in dominant approaches that seek to reform, to repair and to restore faith in the liberal political system. In these managerial and instrumentalising approaches to hope, and as reflected in much of the academic commentary and analysis considered above, this has led to a conflation between the crisis besetting liberal political institutions reliant on a telos of modernist progress, and a crisis of hope more broadly. Analytical philosopher, Katie Stockdale, for example, argues:

> How can we hope to build a just world in the face of so many overlapping forms of oppression that are not going away any time soon? How can we sustain hope in the face of persistent individual, collective, and institutional failures…? How can we hope for just outcomes in the future when injustices in the past have been left unaddressed? Is it even rational to hope under these conditions? And as I struggle with hope from my own position of privilege, I wonder how individuals with far less social and political power than I can hope for change in their own lives within the confines of their oppressions.
>
> (Stockdale 2021, 7)

This concern with the discrediting of the modernist political imaginary neatly captures the mainstream approach to hope as a problem for the liberal order. Hope is required to pick up the slack caused by a breakdown in the usual mechanisms of political activism and the usual liberal imaginary of social and political progress. Hope is called upon to fill in the gaps that enable a telos of liberal improvement to be maintained. If this forward momentum were to stop, apparently – all too apparently – all that would be left would be a world of failed promises, of unbearable inequalities and racialised exploitation. Without hope, we are led to understand that it would be difficult for a liberal analytical philosopher to cope with the disastrousness of the world, let alone someone who may be poor and oppressed.

In fine, there is a problem with the way that hope has been enrolled into supporting liberal assumptions of social and economic progress and in insisting that, what would seem to be a complete exhaustion of the modernist political imagination is merely a blip; a blip that can be overcome with a little more positive thinking and a slight lowering of horizons. Stockdale is not at all alone in the desire to analytically conceive of ways to make hope fungible enough to serve the purposes of continuing to prop up the social, economic and political system that currently exists. A recent book by another analytical philosopher, Maria van der Lugt, *Hopeful Pessimism* (2025) ploughs the same furrow, in thinking about how hope might be adapted to serve the contemporary ends of political repair. Hope needs to fill the vacuum, to be able to ground action that seeks to positively address problems such as climate change, without either falling into the errors of promising too much and leading to burnout and disillusionment (false optimism or 'wishful hope') or, at the opposite extreme, promising too little and providing little encouragement for action (passive pessimism).

The first step, for this governmentalised form of hope, moulded to fit today's needs, is the need to balance consequentialism with a values-based understanding, often expressed as hope 'for' vis-à-vis hope 'in' framings of hope. In this way, it is still possible to ground practices in hope without having a high expectation of success. If virtuous practice, such as active engagement in the struggle for social justice or against climate change, is the key requirement, then this needs to be grounded not so much in a radical outcome but in the values that are worth fighting for. To put it crudely then, 'The point is that hope matters, but it needs to be the right kind of hope—the kind that persists when other versions fail' (2025, xviii). For those who campaign for political repair, hope is understood as a necessary precondition for this.

For analytical philosophers, it appears that it is possible to pick and choose approaches to hope, as if a hope box was arraigned before them and their philosophical training enabled them to pick a hope that best served their required purpose. Hope becomes, in fact, an entirely secondary consideration for writers such as van der Lugt, merely a way of pragmatically grounding action itself:

> The true test is not how hopeful or desperate, how optimistic or pessimistic we are. Either way, there is a risk that it becomes just about words and feelings; that it costs us nothing. The real test is about how our attitudes solidify; in how they come to ground.
>
> (van der Lugt 2025, 198)

Similarly for Stockdale, hope is a secondary support only: 'hope supplements agent's commitments, lending additional motivation to their practical pursuits' (2021, 75); 'when hope supplements our commitments to the most important moral and political ends, it is an especially praiseworthy mental state to sustain in its own right' (Stockdale 2021).

To read analytical philosophers discussing hope, it might appear that hope is so fungible that it can cover anything that is considered to enable action. As many authors point out, the understanding of hope and analysis of its value has been reduced to discussions that are policy-oriented where hope is merely a fungible resource, 'largely instrumental and derivative of consequences' (for example, Thompson 2024, 312). Even reinscribing hope in terms of despair is fine as long as, in desperation, people are driven to act. Of course, arguments that hope could also operate in ways other than those seen to be beneficial are quickly dismissed. For van der Lugt, this would include where 'we could easily imagine radical hope as being the *wrong* response entirely' (2025, 113, italics in original). Accepting climate disaster as already here and hoping to live and to die well in the Anthropocene would be 'deeply misguided' (Thompson 2024). Rather than providing an analysis of hope itself as a mode of working in the world, as a way of holding open futural imaginaries, the emphasis is on the need for hope, for hope's instrumentalisation in the political causes for which the writer advocates.

According, therefore, to climate activist Greta Thunberg, 'No matter how dark things may become, giving up will never be an option' as climate change is a process not a one-off event, 'it will never be too late for us to save as much as we can possibly save'; hope is required not only for now, but 'forever' (cited in van der Lugt 2025, 114). For the analytical philosophers, hope literally can never die by definitional fiat: 'Hoping well involves shifting the target of hope when the world proves to be resistant to some hoped-for end's being realized' (Stockdale 2021, 77). Hope in these readings becomes indistinguishable from a moral duty to do the best, no matter how dark the political prognosis. Stockdale writes: 'there is something morally admirable about... maintaining hopes related to justice in the face of a low chance of success. And what seems admirable about such hopes is that they supplement agents' commitment to their moral ends' (2021, 74). As van der Lugt recognises, this is 'a hope strangely close to hopelessness' (2025, 146).

The flipside of the advocacy of 'good hope' as a moral duty is the denigration of those who do not hope to save this world of disastrousness and denial. According to these philosophers, not having 'good hope' is a privilege that should be checked. As American writer and activist Rebecca Solnit argues, the loss of hope is 'an indulgence if you look at the power of being political as a privilege not granted to everyone' or a product of 'fatigue, a loss of faith, that can be overcome' and addressed, 'hence the need for a kind of education in hope' (2016, 12). Of course, hope is never on behalf of the privileged but always on behalf of others. It is not morally feasible to give up hope:

> ...the point to make is simply a democratic one: it is not up to us (any of us) to decide unilaterally that it's not worth continuing the fight. Climate change is a global problem, whose harms are borne disproportionately

> by the most disenfranchised... No one, least of all those who stand furthest from the front lines of disaster, is entitled to decide on behalf of those most vulnerable that their suffering is not worth fighting for.
> (van der Lugt 2025, 175)

Little seems to have changed since hope was the support act to Christian faith and charity. Analytical philosophy professes a faith in human goodness and the moral duty of charity to others. As Stockdale argues, hope is secondary to an 'intrinsic moral faith: a faith that our lives are worth living and worth fighting for', there is a 'value in struggling against climate injustice as an expression of love for our home and out of our "debt" (or moral duty) to future and previous generations, regardless of the difference these actions ultimately make in the end' (2021, 166).

As Lewis Gordon argues, this view of hope in progress, hope that is invested in *this* world, actually is counter-intuitive in that it reenforces the world as it is, the status quo, at the same time as problematising those who are more vulnerable or marginalised, who are understood to contribute to their own circumstances precisely through their lack of ability or cultural capacity to 'hope well'. As Gordon states: 'The grammatical structure of theodicy, which underlies Euromodern rationalizations of justice in avowed liberal democracies... insists on hope while producing hopeless situations' (Gordon 2024, 159).

HOPE AS AN ETHICOPOLITICAL PRACTICE

Rather than thinking of hope as a resource for the politics and the world that already exists, there is a critical, radical, tradition that draws upon hope in order to think differently and to practice a different kind of politics. Hope as an alternative approach to the political does not seek to build and improve upon what already exists, in denial of the crisis of global warming and the limits of the Anthropocene. Rather than focusing upon filling in the gaps in the world that exists, hope as an alternative ethicopolitical approach struggles to bring otherwise worlds into being through a critique of modernist liberal assumptions and the repressive social order which they underpin (Eagleton 2017, 31–34). The differentiation between the liberal managerial approaches discussed above and more critical approaches to hope is often articulated in terms of hope that is invested in *this* world and hope that seeks to hold open futural possibilities of other possible worlds.

This book analyses but also begins to trouble the binary nature of this distinction between hegemonic and more critical enrolments of hope. Its focus is how, in the contemporary condition, calls for alternative approaches to hope have problematically sought to negotiate the double bind of liberal 'optimism', affirming the world as it exists, and 'utopian' moves of disavowal, operating to deny the structuring context of coloniality and racial capitalism. Hope, as a field of critical thought and resistance, requires further thought and engagement. Engagement which seeks to push back a little on claims that ethicopolitical approaches can escape problems of the liberal managerial capture of hope. While it is clear that hegemonic approaches to hope, as articulated in contemporary analytical philosophy and social psychology, are problematic in their attachments to the existing societal order, this book seeks to analyse and engage alternative imaginaries and approaches that seek to utilise hope in more critical, darker and problematising ways.

The approach to hope that underpinned the politics of liberal modernity, according to Eagleton, should not be overly mourned. This mode of utilising hope was problematic in that, in its ideology of progress, all moments of the past:

> ...are devalued by the fact that each of them is no more than a stepping stone to a successor, the present a mere gangplank to the future. Every point of time is diminished in relation to an infinity of points still to

> come... [A prospect] that strips human history of its catastrophic character... [and is thereby] both morally complacent and politically quietist.
>
> (Eagleton 2017, 31–32)

Hegemonic understandings of hope therefore regarded previous history as 'dead and done' while the future was viewed as always 'open and indeterminate', full of infinite possibility. As Elizabeth Povinelli correctly argues, it is crucial 'to remember the function of the horizon and frontier in liberalism as a mechanism of disavowal' (2021, 38). Modernist hope, in this way, was very much a secularised version of Christian hope, playing second fiddle to 'faith', recast in Enlightenment terms of scientific rationalism rather than the coming of the Kingdom of God. For Adam Potkay, 'what we now think of as political hope—hope in the socially transformative power of representative government... is arguably, a product of the French Revolution' (2024, 60). This was a romantic Wordworth-inspired hope of a new secular beginning with rational Man at the centre, giving meaning to the world as it lay infinitely open before us.

An example of hope that is invested in *this* world would be Wendell Berry's approach, very much in the tradition of Immanuel Kant, where hope requires us to act 'as if' the world was not one of disastrousness, genocide and racial exclusion:

> I will not be optimistic, for its [humanity as a whole] history is full of ugliness and cruelty and violence and waste; it has inflicted terrible damage on itself and on the world. But I will be steadfastly hopeful, for as a member of the human race I am also in the company of men... who through all the sad destructive centuries of our history have kept alive the vision of peace and kindness and generosity and humility and freedom.
>
> (Wendell Berry cited in Lamb 2024, 373, n.68)

Berry expresses hope in the liberal telos of progressive politics, whereas this book is concerned with an examination of hope as it is deployed to underpin alternative ethicopolitical imaginaries, premised upon the critique of the present rather than the desire to extend it into the future. Hope invoked as an alternative ethicopolitical practice refuses the 'Euromodern grammar' of hope on the basis that, rather than having hope in the future as a disavowal of the present, the present itself is the basis of a futural potentiality of otherwise worlds.

Perhaps the key theorist associated with hope as a mode of ethicopolitical engagement itself is Ernst Bloch, who articulated hope as essential to the human condition, not a mental attitude of optimism or positivity or the desperateness of pessimism but rather a processual becoming (1986). As Eagleton argues:

> Hope, like desire as such, is the way in which the human animal is nonidentical with itself, its existence an eternal not-yet, its substance a kind of suspension. It represents... 'a basic modality of human existence', not simply a mental attitude.
>
> (Eagleton 2017, 44)

Hope, as a way of framing an ethicopolitical mode of activity, is assumed to be more than purely an act of wishful thinking – an 'abstract utopia' – but grounded in the present, in practices of becoming otherwise (Danewid 2024; Kelley 2022). It is hope's underpinning of understandings of human potentiality that enables emancipatory or liberatory projects, working against the blockages to their becoming. Eagleton writes:

> To realise one's inner being involves not just breaking ecstatically through a set of external barriers, but the rather more exacting business of emancipating ourselves from ourselves. We need to reeducate our desires, not just externalise them freely... Whereas desire for Freud is always in some sense botched and perverse, Bloch treats it in the form of hope as unequivocally positive. Negativity is largely a question of hindrance.
>
> (Eagleton 2017, 101–102)

Hope can therefore be enabling for alternative ethicopolitical projects strongly connected with human life itself, with conatus, with vitality, with the way that life finds a way out of no way; the way in which life is held to be a creative force in excess of liberal regimes of representation. It is this desire that enables the utilisation of hope for critical approaches that view the modern condition as one in which humanity is alienated both from itself and from the world. From this perspective, the present is always lacking, unfinished and imperfectly realised, always 'Not-Yet' in a Blochian terminology (Eagleton 2017, 104). Bloch is a central theorist for alternative approaches to hope; his work has been adapted by commentators and theorists working across a number of critical traditions, drawn to the ways in which Bloch centred indeterminacy and the power of human agency and creativity (Gulliford 2024, 212). Bloch's understanding of hope focused less on specific and potentially achievable ends and more upon anticipation, on the opening up to experiences that problematise what exists in the present, that are driven by its lack, 'by what is missing' and in this critical rejection seek to 'critically negate the negative' that is *this* world (Webb 2024, 286).

In this sense, ethicopolitical imaginaries that draw upon hope can be read as 'doubly critical', in that they are critical of an unfulfilled present but also critical of any claims of ready-made solutions or closures to the process of becoming otherwise (Webb 2024, 287). Hope thereby works very differently here than when enlisted in support of formal state-based or reform-oriented political party projects and programmes. This alternative ethicopolitical tradition of critical thought and practice, of open-ended and self-making freedom, can be traced through the Black radical tradition (see Robinson 2000) and can be seen across a range of non-traditional or marginalised experiences of struggle. These struggles are often expressed and theorised outside the constraints of liberal institutions, for example, in the 'undercommons' rather than in civil society (Harney and Moten 2013), and outside a representational politics of essentialised identities. As Lia Haro notes, hope underpins ethicopolitical practices that work much more along the lines of the Zapatistas project which seeks to deterritorialise traditional political projects and to create 'alternative horizons of possibility' (cited in Webb 2024, 286–287).

Hope is thereby crucial for critical modes of political understanding and of ethicopolitical practice, which focus neither upon state power nor economic transformation designed to overcome social and economic divisions. Hope is utilised for the opening and enabling of alternative futures, involving the work of the subject itself upon both the external world, its relations to others and, perhaps most importantly, the subject's relationship to itself. Hope, in these ways, is claimed to enable work that challenges the repressive constraints of modernist constructions of the world and their temporal imaginaries of closure. Hope thereby informs modes of ethicopolitical praxis driven by the desire for freedom understood as a process, as negation, rather than freedom as the fulfilment of some idealised goal or specific end (of socialism or communism, for example). Thus, hope is central to the struggles and analytics of ethicopolitical approaches that seek to maintain the aspirations of critique and present themselves as a far cry from naïve expressions of positivity and the affirmation of what already exists.

THIS BOOK

This book analyses the content and dynamics of contemporary utilisations of hope to underpin ethicopolitical projects seeking to hold futures open. These operate within and against the closures of this broken world, cognisant not merely of the disastrousness of climate change but also of the end of *this* world as a predictable and controllable background to human action. In this way, hope informs alternative political imaginaries which structure a relational ethicopolitical approach whereby futural, more enabling, modes of being, or becoming 'human' are articulated, without the cuts and separations of formal 'politics' which operates in a strict 'top-down' manner. Thus, hope is increasingly enrolled within ethicopolitical praxes, modes of being, practicing and experimenting, that seek to bring into being a 'reality' that exists beyond the appearance of the world. It is for this reason that hope can be held to be critical: by definitional fiat, it is utilised to go beyond the world as given.

Chapter 1, 'Libidinal Drives' analyses the centrality of the human subject to radical ethicopolitical imaginaries underpinned by hope. One important way into this analysis is via the work of the Frankfurt School theorists in developing and challenging Sigmund Freud's analysis of the human unconscious. In this framing, the human as an ethicopolitical subject is always exorbitant to and in excess of realms of liberal representation, which abstract from private, psychological and physiological aspects of the individual. It is this repressed realm of the unconscious, of libidinal drives and desires, which is held to provide radical futural possibilities and potentialities. While the modern liberal order is based upon the repression and control of pre-existing dynamic drives, powers, capacities and desires, radical change and transformation can be premised on their enablement. This chapter thereby traces attempts to articulate alternative potentialities on the basis of these immanent generative powers and capacities, through to Hardt and Negri's understanding of 'multitude' and Fred Moten's para-ontological framing of Black sociality.

'Freedom Dreams', Chapter 2, engages approaches to hope which rather than focusing upon enabling the repressed inner drives and desires of the subject, instead work on the possibilities of thinking differently, of liberating the mind from the constrictive categories of hegemonic thought. There is an initial engagement with the

Kantian tradition of work on aesthetics as key to breaking the individual from the immediacy of the world. Engagement with hope as a matter of 'freeing the mind' is illustrated by an analysis of the work of Cedric Robinson and the Black radical tradition and the processual understanding of 'abolition' as open-ended rather than goal directed. The chapter concludes with a discussion of Neil Roberts' concept of 'marronage' and Michi Saagiig Nishnaabeg scholar, Leanne Betsamosake Simpson's conception of 'grounded normativity' where autonomy increasingly lies in the means, in the process of becoming otherwise, rather than in the immediate or final ends.

Chapter 3 critically engages with 'worlding', as a third mode of utilising hope within alternative ethicopolitical praxes. While the human as subject is still central to this approach, processual becoming is focused less on 'liberating' the mind or the imagination and more on removing barriers to responsivity and receptivity. The openness of processual becoming is a worldly one, suborning the human to the world understood as lively and in flux. It is these worldly relations, particularly the relations of care to communities, to nature, and the environment, that need to come to the fore. Thus, this form of enhancing 'autonomy' is a highly responsibilising one, where the terms of becoming are relational rather than set by the human subject itself. Worlding, as underpinned by hope, as a mode of ethicopolitical engagement and critique, appears closely aligned with international policy discourses of resilience and adaptation. These similarities are drawn out, and attention is placed on the problem of ontological ambiguity, which means that alternative ethicopolitical praxes informed by hope can appear caught between idealism and essentialising the world as it exists.

'Hope against Hope', Chapter 4, foregrounds the problem of 'ontological ambiguity' whereby the enrolment of hope in struggles to hold open alternative futures can unintentionally reproduce the problems of liberal and exclusionary discourses of progress, either falling into the trap of optimism (apologia) or utopianism (disavowal). In making this point, this chapter highlights ways in which the enrolling of hope within these projects risks affirmation of the world and the subject as constituted in modernity. The chapter then analyses how the utilisation of hope has been problematised in attempts to disarticulate the subject to avoid the ontological trap of essentialising and responsibilising marginalised groups. The second half of the chapter illustrates 'hope against hope' via a brief consideration of 'Queer negativity', 'Crip negativity' and 'Black nihilism', approaches that seek to stay with the disastrousness of the world rather than move to disavow it.

Critical thought has increasingly turned to hope in the struggle to hold open otherwise worlds. Without hope it would be necessary to confront the disastrousness of *this* world rather than articulate futures that necessarily evade or disavow it. To make this point, the concluding chapter, firstly highlights the limits of much of the critical work that seeks to problematise the governmentalisation of hope. It suggests that this, predominantly Foucauldian, problematisation fails to engage more broadly with hope's ontological limitations. While the biopolitical critique relies on hope being instrumentalised as a tool of power, this book moves beyond this critique to problematise the ontological assumptions grounding hope and underpinning the ethicopolitical critiques that seek to imagine other possible worlds in the present. In doing so, the concluding chapter engages with Marc Augé's *The Future* (2014) to emphasise the centrality of humanism to hope and closes with a brief reading of Louise Amoore's *Cloud Ethics* (2020) where the exorbitance of the human and the plenitude of the world necessarily provides the unacknowledged grounds for critical imaginaries of hope today.

NOTES

1 A quote that Mark Fisher originally attributed to philosophers Fredric Jameson and Slavoj Žižek (Fisher 2014, 2).

2 A trope often attributed to science-fiction writer, William Gibson. On the uneven distribution of the future and the importance of realising that there are many ‘ends of the world’, some of them already in the past, see for example, Danowski and Viveiros de Castro (2017).

PART ONE

REENCHANTING THE HUMAN

1

LIBIDINAL DRIVES

INTRODUCTION

The desire to enrol hope within struggles against the multiple closures of broken worlds has, from its inception, been driven by disillusionment with the exclusionary and failing processes, structures and outcomes of liberal modernity. For earlier critical theorists, the closing off of the future was all too real in the experience of totalitarianism, the industrial violence of the Holocaust, and the atomic bombs unleashed over Hiroshima and Nagasaki, and, for later theorists, on account of the collapse of traditional left projects and the closures of global climate change. In fine, whether hope has the capacity to hold open the possibility of alternative futures, becomes an important question as increasingly broken worlds highlight humanity's failure to deliver on the promises of progress, reason and human equality (see Bargués et al 2024).

It should be noted that the attraction to ethicopolitical approaches, underpinned by hope, is not merely based upon disillusionment; there is also a positive and affirmative sense in which holding open futures seems more important than searching for finalities and closures. In a world in which unintended consequences are seen to be more important than intended ones and where externalities and unaccounted impacts continue to reverberate, we are less likely to see problems as discrete and separable (see Chandler et al 2021). This is a world that appears to

DOI: 10.4324/9781003632719-3

no longer fit modernist framings of linear histories and imaginaries of universal logics of capital, 'there is no iron law of necessity in history' (Banerjee and Wouters 2022, 46; see also Chandler 2018) or 'unilinear progression' (Robinson 2019, 119). It is then not merely disillusionment but also a sense that modernist understandings and approaches to problem-solving and the rush to resolve, rather than to 'stay with the problem', can be counterproductive (Haraway 2016). Hope is thereby increasingly utilised to constitute a different mode of ethicopolitical praxis as modernist imaginaries of fixed subjects and goals dissolve in a 'dialectics without determinism' (Gordon 2019, xxiv; see also Wynter n.d.).

This approach of holding open the future rather than seeking closures and certainties runs counter to the abstraction and reductionism of liberal and Marxist political theories – their 'capitalcentrism' and their fetishisation of industrial labour (the proletariat). Hope utilised to inform a futural response to the closures of broken worlds is ethicopolitically grounded in alternative more marginalised modes of struggle (Robinson 2019, 118) seen to inculcate new ways of enabling communities and imagining the world, and of remaking the subject or forging a 'new genre' of the human (Wynter 2003). This usage of hope can also be seen to register a shift from a universal 'world' to a world of 'many worlds' (de la Cadena and Blaser 2018; Bradley 2023), a world where modes of becoming are conceived as multiple (Mignolo 2018a; Viveiros de Castro 2014) and struggles against hegemony are seen to be less mediated via representative institutions (Hardt and Negri 2000). Thus, ethicopolitical struggles tend not to be generalisable. As Hardt and Negri have observed, diverse struggles in their radical attention to autonomy and refusal, lack mediation, they lack a universalisable or a 'communicable' aspect (2000, 54–55; Spivak 1994).[1]

This chapter analyses some of the ways in which hope is enrolled to underpin critical approaches which focus upon resistance to repression articulated via bodily, affective, unconscious, libidinal or desiring aspects of human agency. Working with and against Freud, the human is imagined as a divided subject, always non-identical with itself, always already in the process of becoming other than itself (Eagleton 2017, 44). Powerfully formulated in the work of Herbert Marcuse in the 1950s, the emphasis on libidinal drives and desires was later revived by the autonomous Marxist Antonio Negri, who has done much to bring processual understandings of the subject into the mainstream of political thinking. Evading, or 'in flight from', formal institutional politics of states, hope underpins the analysis of radical becoming that thereby keeps open alternative futures that are grounded in the present, always understood as in-formation (Banerjee and Wouters 2022, 65). The second half of this chapter engages the work of Sylvia Wynter on the 'overrepresentation of Man', particularly her earlier work, *Black Metamorphosis* (n.d.), on the promise of Black diasporic becoming in the absence of fixed identities and Fred Moten's extension of this analysis on hope and Black sociality. It then discusses the understanding of futural becoming in Jose Muñoz's *Cruising Utopia* (2019) and Robert McRuer's work on critical disability. These examples demonstrate in differing ways how the enrolment of hope is fundamental to projects of open futurity, on the basis of the understanding of the subject as engaged in struggle as an open-ended process of self-making.

HOPE AND REPRESSION

Hope is utilised very differently in alternative ethicopolitical imaginaries in comparison to the narrowly instrumentalised hope discussed in the policy-related fields of psychology and analytical philosophy. This alternative mode of hope's enrolment can be seen to have several intellectual roots, the most important, perhaps, is the critical tradition of the Frankfurt School, where hope plays a central role, with differing emphases present, in the work of Ernst Bloch, Theodore Adorno and Herbert Marcuse, amongst others. For theorists working in the critical tradition, hope was closely associated with a form of critique that attempted to keep alternative futures open in struggle against the theoretical and political repression of industrial modernity. These theorists sought to rely not upon the pragmatics of 'scientific realism' but rather the negentropic power of the 'life instincts' (Marcuse 1987, 22).[2] If the closed and alienated condition of modernity stemmed from the bureaucratic rationalisation of existence, then it followed that attempts to break from this appealed to powers that were understood to operate outside of these constraints.

A different articulation of the 'human', beyond the abstract, rationalist, framing of liberal universalism, was central to this utilisation of hope. This included paying attention to the importance of psychological, cultural, libidinal and affective realms in the construction of subjectivity. In Eurocentric analyses, this approach comes into focus with the work of Freud, and attention to the unconscious as a realm of freedom, one that (for Freud) needs 'civilising', or taming, repressing problematic natural urges and desires held to be disruptive. The Frankfurt School then reworked understandings of the unconscious as a reserve of futural potentiality and radical enablement. Thus, psychoanalytical understandings became central to critique and discourses of liberation. Freedom was no longer merely a formal political concept, associated with democratic and civil rights, but also a project which utilised hope to envisage alternative modes of being and open-ended processes of agential becoming.

Perhaps the key work which underpins what might be called the alternative 'standard model' of hope is Herbert Marcuse's *Eros and Civilization: A Philosophical Inquiry into Freud*, first published in 1955 (1987). The essential assumption of modernist thought (as discussed in the Introduction) is that history is progress, that the development of technologies and the sciences lead to higher and higher levels of civilisation, and that whatever the errors, tragedies and mistakes along the way, lessons will be learned, and life will be improved for all. It is on the basis of this assumption (that history = progress = civilisation) that the modern state acquires the capacities for coercion and control, in the realms of policing and the military but also in the social and educational realms. The politics of the left and the right that shaped modernity, since the French Revolution, shared the key assumptions of modernist thought, merely disagreeing over which methods and levers of control were more efficient, markets or states. Marcuse's work, along with that of others associated with the Frankfurt School of critical theory, was a response to a growing disillusionment with these modernist assumptions of progress.[3]

While the socialist and communist left wanted to take modernity further in the direction of the development of science and technology and bureaucratic rationality, as a replacement for market forces, theorists linked to the Frankfurt School were sceptical of claims to state-based rationality and direction. Instead of pushing for top-down modes of transformation, Marcuse turned to human instincts, questioning Freud's view that these needed to be tamed and subjugated as part of the process of civilisation and modernisation. The culture of modernity, for Marcuse, was built on the repression of instinctual needs: 'The methodological sacrifice of libido, its rigidly enforced deflection to socially useful activities and expressions, *is* culture' (1987, 3 italics in original) he bemoaned. Modernity was not a higher stage of civilisation, merely a more sophisticated mode of repression, where human drives and desires (the *pleasure principle*) become the basis upon which society is suborned to the needs of capitalist profitability and technological productivity (the *reality principle*) (1987, 12).

In essence, Freud's analysis of the unconscious as 'ruled by the pleasure principle' provides a reserve to be drawn upon, available historically and structurally prior to the imposition by the modernisation process of the 'reality principle' (the acceptance of modernist modes of being as somehow natural). This drive is understood to be both phylogenetically prior (over the history of human evolution) and ontogenetically prior (over the life of the individual); the process of 'civilisation' over history being mirrored by the process of socialisation in childhood. On both levels, the struggle to control and repress natural drives, to suborn them to the requirements of social order, is one that requires continuous reproduction and thus is 'never complete and never secure' (Marcuse 1987, 15).

It is this struggle over the libidinal drives that shapes the history of different modes of governance and, because it is a continual process, contingent and contested, provides the material grounds for hope as a distinct mode of practice:

> In Freudian terms, is the conflict between pleasure principle and reality principle irreconcilable to such a degree that it necessitates the repressive transformation of man's instinctual structure? Or does it allow the concept of a non-repressive civilization, based on a fundamentally different experience of being, a fundamentally different relation between man and nature, and fundamentally different existential relations?
>
> (Marcuse 1987, 5)

Freud's analysis of the libidinal drives and their location in the unconscious thus provides a source of ethicopolitical critique that expands the locus of political struggle from control over the mechanisms of political power and economic production to also include the struggle over the human psyche. This point is fundamental to the discussion in the chapters that follow, so it is worth quoting Marcuse's reading of Freud on this point:

> ... ever since the first, prehistoric restoration of domination following the first rebellion, repression from

> without has been supported by repression from within: the unfree individual introjects his masters and their commands into his own mental apparatus. The struggle against freedom reproduces itself in the psyche of man, as the self-repression of the repressed individual, and his self-repression in turn sustains his masters and their institutions. It is this mental dynamic which Freud unfolds as the dynamic of civilization.
>
> (Marcuse 1987, 16)

However, this subjugation is never complete; modernity is haunted by the ongoing societal repression of human needs and desires. While developed consciousness may be capable of sublimating the human drive to live in the 'absence of want and repression', this potential can be unlocked through freeing our imaginations, enabling our unconscious, repressed, libidinal desires: 'An innermost tendency in the organism militates against the principle which has governed civilization and insists on return from alienation' (Marcuse 1987, 109). For Freud, the unconscious could only provide a primal or premodern, retrogressive imaginary, rooted in the past, but for Marcuse, and for hope as ethicopolitical praxis, 'such a principle could itself become a historical reality, a matter of developing consciousness… the images of phantasy could refer to the unconquered *future* of mankind rather than to its (badly) conquered past' (1987, 147 italics in original):

> The truth value of imagination relates not only to the past but also to the future: the forms of freedom and happiness which it invokes claim to deliver the historical *reality*. In its refusal to accept as final the limitations imposed upon freedom and happiness by the reality principle, in its refusal to forget what *can* be, lies the critical function of phantasy.
>
> (Marcuse 1987, 148–149 italics in original)

Thus, hope informs an ethicopolitical praxis of holding open the future which seeks to draw upon these libidinal desires for freedom. This negation of what *is* is not a regressive desire to return to the past but emerges against the constraints of the present which are largely mental rather than material (as the development of civilisation means material happiness should be possible for all). Liberating inner passions and desires, rather than exploiting, controlling and repressing them, would then enable other worlds to be possible, worlds beyond the modernist imaginary, constituting new modes of being human, which do not depend upon competition, exploitation and degradation:

> The opposition between man and nature, subject and object, is overcome. Being is experienced as gratification, which unites man and nature so that the fulfilment of the man is at the same time the fulfilment, without violence, of nature... the things of nature become free to be what they are. But to be what they are they *depend* on the erotic attitude: they receive their *telos* only in it.
>
> (Marcuse 1987, 166)

Hope is here enrolled for the work of holding open alternative and open-ended futurities which rest upon the development of the internal capacities and capabilities of the human as transformative and world-making subject, a subject capable of collective individuation through processes of open-ended love and care. For Marcuse, central to these alternative ethicopolitical praxes was installing an 'order of sensuousness as against the order of reason' (1987, 190). The human subject would then be an enabling and differentiating one, giving expression to 'the "inner life" of its objects' and enabling 'the free manifestation of potentialities' (Marcuse 1987). Thus, in a reversal of the modern political ontology: 'Freedom would have to be sought in the liberation of the sensuousness rather than reason, and in the limitation of the "higher" faculties in favor of the "lower"'(Marcuse 1987).

Although non-rationalist, as stated, hope was not utilised in the 'abstract' terms of naïve wishful thinking, but grounded, in the sense that it drew upon the potentiality of the present rather than what is given in immediate appearance. It is an awareness, as Bertolt Brecht states, that 'Something's missing' (Bloch and Adorno 1988, 15). Hope is used to underpin a radical processual understanding of the potentiality of the desiring libidinal subject itself, enabling its own agency, its own work of struggle. As Ernst Bloch argued:

> Hope is not confidence. If it could not be disappointed, it would not be hope. That is part of it. Otherwise, it would be cast in a picture. It would let itself be bargained down. It would capitulate and say, that is what I had hoped for.
>
> (Bloch and Adorno 1988, 16)

Likewise, hope cannot have a goal, something to be achieved in the world (as it exists). As Adorno states, once goals are realised, they no longer perform the critical futural function of hope:

> As they have been realized, the dreams themselves have assumed a peculiar character of sobriety, of the spirit of positivism, and beyond that, of boredom. What I mean by this is that it is not simply a matter of presupposing that what really is has limitations as opposed to that which has infinitely imaginable possibilities. Rather, I mean something concrete, namely, that one sees oneself almost always deceived: the fulfillment of the wishes takes something away from the substance of the wishes, as in the fairy tale [where three wishes are granted by the Djinn released from a bottle]...
>
> (Bloch and Adorno 1988, 1)

'Something is missing' in this world as it is grasped through hegemonic discourses of repressive control. However, this is not a concrete or tangible thing to be attained (as in the 'standard model' of hope, discussed in the introductory chapter). What is missing is the possibility to become otherwise in an unalienated way. It is through the struggle to become otherwise, to follow passions and desires which are constrained and repressed, that alternative futures will be held open against the closures of broken worlds. In this respect, a continuation of the work of Marcuse and the post-Marxism of the Frankfurt School can be seen developed in the work of the late Italian philosopher and autonomous Marxist, Antonio Negri.

This is particularly true of Negri's articulation of the constituent power of the multitude which he counterposed to the repressive power of the modern state (1999). Here, the post-Freudian analogy between the 'multitude' and the libidinal subject is clear:

> Constituent power is therefore the passion of the multitude.... The movement of constituent power is indefatigable... The plot of the constitution of the political here is sustained by the unstoppable and progressive expansion of *cupiditas* [desire], which is the determinate force in the constitution of the social, determinate in the formation of the political institutions... Precisely by considering the contradictions and conflicts of the passions as background of the process, constituent power is realized as a tendency. It is continually reopened and defined as absolute in its reopening. It exists in reality, it exists in war and crisis, but this is the divinity of the world.
>
> (Negri 1999, 304)

For Negri, the constituent power of the multitude explodes the separation between the political sphere and the social: 'The project is no longer that of making the political coincide with the social, but that of inserting the production of the political into the creation of the social' (1999, 306). It is a constantly creative power of life, of becoming against closure and constraint, 'an affirmation – of strength, the revolution, the concrete against the abstract, what is living against what is cold, alienated, inert, and fixed' (1999, 307).

It is important to note here the ontological continuity with the critical tradition in the historical and logical prioritisation of the libidinal and desiring creative and productive powers of the subject which necessarily come before attempts by power to control, to regulate and to direct this power. It is this immanent 'life force' which is key to hope's utilisation in alternative ethicopolitical imaginaries which operate to disrupt and to problematise political closure:

> To take this element away from the political means to take everything away from it; it means to reduce it to pure administrative and diplomatic mediation, to bureaucratic and police activity – that is, exactly to that against which constituent power, as origin of the political, continually struggles in order to emerge as strength... constituent power comes first, it is the definition itself of the political, and where it is repressed and excluded, the political is reduced to pure mechanical nature, to being an enemy, and a despotic power. (Negri 1999, 334)

In this way, hope is held to enable approaches that seek to remain true to the vibrancy of the world, holding it open, rather than setting themselves up against it, as separate from it. Hope is put to work in a very different register to that of the liberal political imaginary of state-level bargaining and representative competition. As Negri asserts: 'constituent power has nothing to do with natural rights theory' (1999, 308): '... throughout its history constituent power presents itself as radically and continually in opposition to natural right theory: creation against contract, and vitality and innovation against order and hierarchy' (Negri 1999). Constituent power is very much reliant on hope to inform ethicopolitical praxis because it underpins the promise that other worlds are possible and prefigured in the struggles within this one.[4]

As Negri states: 'constituent power by continuing to live as strength and reorganize itself as multitude presents itself as the paradigm of a temporal dimension open into the future' (1999, 311). If constitutionalism represents the political closures of the modern state form, then constituent power is the refusal of closure and faith in the multitude's own 'radical immanence', its self-governing capabilities as a community in the process of becoming against constitutionalism and its attempts to police and to impose order and hierarchy (Negri 1999, 321).

For Negri, the multitude are an expression of the constitutive libidinal force of life itself. He describes two 'ontological levels', the natural and the social. Firstly, the development of the human being itself, the 'first ontological level, on which is inscribed the progressive passage of passions, imagination, and intelligence toward higher and higher degrees of ontological density' (1999, 322). Secondly, the specifically human mode of development: '... when, ethically, love and joy break the continual rhythm of the ontological process... Constituent power has completely liberated itself, in its positive determination, as determination of the ontological fabric and as its creative overdetermination' (1999, 322). Life, specifically human life, becomes self-determining at this second ontological level, 'the first pertains to natural human history and the second determines a destiny of human liberation' (Negri 1999). Hope enables this material grounding in the human as a self-making subject, thus: 'the break between necessity and freedom is inserted into ontology; it defines ontology and explains its permanence, progressive enrichment, and innovative strength' (Negri 1999).

Hope enables this project of holding the future open because it requires grounding in the immanent constitutive power of life as expressed through the human, organised in communities of creative, social, modes of self-making differentiation. Thus, the subject of history is not individuals, or really collectivities, but rather the virtual, libidinal, agency of constituent power itself. This power is not in itself progressive; it is an immanent drive which comes up against limits and constraints. This libidinal drive is therefore at the heart of the struggle between modernity's drive to limit and constrain constitutive power and emancipatory forces who seek to enable and direct it (1999, 323). Either libidinal drives are contained and redirected by modernity as a totalising closure that 'assumes human and collective creativity in order to insert them into the instrumental rationality of the capitalist mode of production of the world' (Negri 1999), or constituent power negates the rationalising order which seeks to objectify and to instrumentalise the power of the living.

Negri's break from Marxism as a modernist project of top-down control and instrumental rationality follows the insights of the critical tradition in seeking to establish an alternative political imaginary grounded in the constituent or libidinal powers of life itself and the human subject in its collective capacity and desire for freedom. Negri's framing of the multitude as the metaphor for self-making communities that cannot be bound by regimes of representation is a useful framework to think with a wide range of contemporary critical approaches to hope which take the Frankfurt School reworking of Freud to articulate modes of becoming and self-making outside and against the multiple closures of broken worlds. As Achille Mbembe argues, 'in every human subject there is something indomitable and fundamentally intangible that no domination—no matter what form it takes—can eliminate, contain, or suppress, at least not completely' (2017, 170).

BLACKNESS BEYOND REPRESENTATION

For Negri, the radical nature of ethicopolitical struggle underpinned by hope lies in the capacity this provides for the refusal of political parties, programmes and formal political institutions of representation and state power.

Hope enables approaches which seek to harness libidinal powers that operate outside and in excess of regimes of repression and control. Approaches which utilise hope in this way insist that power comes from below, from the people, the multitude, not via abstraction and representation but via experiential, lived, desiring modes of becoming, through open-ended struggles for the world to be otherwise. The late Sylvia Wynter, celebrated writer and scholar of the colonial and postcolonial condition, in her unpublished magnum opus *Black Metamorphosis* (n.d.), stresses a similar break from deterministic Marxism and insists on the underestimated importance of cultural norms in the struggle to keep open alternative futures.

In terms that are closely analogous to Marcuse's articulation of the unconscious as a libidinal drive that pre-exists repressive modernity, Wynter centres the struggle against the 'colonisation of black desire' and the alienation this produces (n.d., 618, 798) in terms of a racial struggle in which a 'cultural reserve' was maintained by Africans shipped as chattel slaves to the Caribbean plantations (n.d., 84). This 'cultural reserve' operated underneath formal and rationalist societal processes of the plantation that sought to reduce African slaves to a less-than-human status. This reserve then acted as a 'subsoil able to take in stronger elements and to reinvent itself' (Wynter n.d.). As expressed in the creativity of Black slave culture in the Americas, this libidinal power worked otherwise to hegemonic world views:

> What the Jokunno masquerade and all later popular black culture represented and represents, is an alternative way of thought, one in which the mind and the senses coexist, where the mind 'feels' and the senses become theoreticians. And black culture then and now remains the neo-popular, neo-native culture of the disrupted. It coexisted and coexists, with the 'rational' plantation system but is in constant danger of destruction.
>
> (Wynter n.d., 109)

Where other exiles came to the Americas with their identities intact, towards a 'land of dreams' or 'manifest destiny', 'the African sailed, packed together, so many piezas [pieces] of labor power, towards a nightmare' (Wynter n.d., 58). Of all the peoples coming to the New World, the African was the only one cut off from the past, from previous cultures and communities; European migrants remained culturally and traditionally attached to their home countries (Wynter n.d., 61). The struggle to be human on the plantation provision grounds involved a creative experimentation developing new cultural forms of community life: 'In order to remain human the multi-tribal African, though shipped as merchandise, would have to invent for himself a new identity' (Wynter n.d., 64). As tribal orthodoxies melted away, a new orthodoxy developed, driven by oral cultural codes, in which change and adaptation were central:

> Of all the emigrants who came to the New world, (the) blacks were, as a group, the most creative culturally. They were the only ones involved in a unique cultural process by which old roots were transplanted into new soil, in the context of a totally alienated experience. They were creative because they had to be. They were the only emigrants who came not as free men towards the American dream of freedom based on the rights of property, but as slaves, as a commodity, as property. From the beginning, then, they constituted the dark underside of the American dream, their existence criticizing its consciousness, their reality the negation of its ideals.
>
> (Wynter n.d., 23–24)

Sylvia Wynter utilises hope to argue that this open-ended culture, of resistance to the dominant reality, operated at 'a deep psychic level' such that: 'Black culture is a reminder that the senses are a part of being and that the murder of the senses is the murder of self' (Wynter n.d., 114). The experience of being Black in the New World generated a counter-cultural disposition which necessitated adaptation but also resistance, a process Wynter calls 'indigenisation' as a principle of liberation. The value of this understanding – where those racialised as Black have an unasked-for advantage in that they lack fixed identities and are forced to adapt to their surroundings in new and creative ways – is that it provides an alternative to the ethnic pluralism of American identity construction. Wynter thus refers to the 'cultural underlife of the black world' (Wynter n.d., 425). Ethnic pluralism operated to enforce 'homogenizing cultural norms', 'centred on a hierarchical arrrangements of plural groups' (Wynter n.d., 854), closing and freezing identities from the top-down. In distinction, hope underpinned an ethicopolitical mode of struggle that worked plurally from the bottom-up:

> The revolt of each group against its own colonized consciousness was the first movement of social liberation... a revolution that could not be fought by proxy, by a vanguard, since it called for the participatory, movement of subversion against one's own internalized variant of the hegemonic ruling consciousness.
>
> (Wynter n.d., 823)

This struggle of becoming against hegemonic closures worked very differently from struggles for ethnic representation, the politics of recognition and of identity, so central to the divisive pluralist paradigm of American liberalism. Blacks were not an 'ethnic group', but a sociocultural group constructed as 'deviant' through societal alienation and struggle in a 'White' social environment (Wynter n.d., 841, 864). Hope thereby informed alternative modes of becoming, that were open-ended and oppositional to the reality as given, and was necessarily key to this Black experiential struggle: 'Blacks were the only group who were to be involved in a sustained popular cultural micro-activity which metamorphosed a former culture into a new one – one that was at one and the same time "ethnic" and American' (Wynter n.d., 866). Wynter argues that 'black culture represented and constituted an alternative mode of culture – a popular American cultural code as opposed to normative American culture in its bourgeoise modality' (Wynter n.d., 867); an 'opposed mode of culture' (Wynter n.d., 884). Blacks, for this reason, were the only social group that could hold open a shared future, that could 'realize America as America – rather than as White Western America' (Wynter n.d., 931). It is through the struggle of openness against closure that Black struggle becomes capable of forming a new social totality, one that problematises hierarchical distinctions and divisions.

For Wynter, this struggle to overcome racial capitalism's societal and political divisions necessarily implied the construction of a 'new genre of the human' against the 'overrepresentation of Man' in the Eurocentric modernist image of the autonomous rational subject of political reason and civil society based upon 'African enslavement, Latin American conquest, and Asian subjugation' (2003, 263). Wynter argues that the modern state and the carving out of an abstract sphere of political equality and rights, which disavowed racial, gender and social exclusions and inequalities, was enabled only through 'the invention of Man' who was to become the political subject of the state (2003, 263) and the subject of a racialised hierarchy of understanding. This hierarchy, rationalised around the abstraction of Man as a political subject, the separation of the spheres of the political (of equality) from the social and economic (spheres where inequality was clear), and a racialised understanding of difference, was therefore constitutive of the 'world' of liberal modernity.

Wynter sees hope as central to Black struggle, as a mode of becoming otherwise, and of reenchanting the human. Building on this rendering of Black hope and Black sociality, American cultural theorist Fred Moten has developed upon the disruptive promise of Black struggle as an attempt to hold off the multiple closures of this world. In this case, the libidinal 'reserve' very much mirrors Negri's articulation of an originary drive that pre-exists attempts of repression and control. Moten makes a 'paraontological' distinction (2013, 749) between Blackness as a concept at the nexus of the social and the ontological and the experiential struggle of people racialised as Black. This paraontological separation seeks to prevent a slippage between fixed or essentialised understandings of identity and a structural problematic of exclusion. This does not deny that there is a close connection between struggles of Black and diasporic African peoples against their 'radical exclusion' from the political order – a world of fixed identities and political positionalities – and 'radical relegation to the social' (2013, 739–740). The key point for Moten's 'Black optimism' is the emphasis on the potentiality of political exclusion and alternative modes of becoming that are in excess of liberal modernity's construction of the political subject and binary divide between the political and the social.

Thus, Moten writes:

> Social death is not imposed upon blackness by or from the standpoint or positionality of the political; rather, *it is the field of the political*, from which blackness is relegated to the supposedly undifferentiated mass or blob of the social...
>
> (Moten 2013, 740)

For Moten it, 'is not just that blackness is ontologically prior to the logistic and regulative power that is supposed to have brought it into existence but that blackness is prior to ontology' (2013, 739). Blackness, as distinct from Black people, is a sociality that is prior to the imposition of a modern liberal ontology of divisions and hierarchy in the sense that this is the necessarily excluded and disavowed 'Other' or outside to the world of Man, the world of the liberal subject and the world limned by the political as a constrained and reductive sphere through which social contestation is managed. This radical disjunction between Black sociality and the state-sanctioned sphere of the liberal subject of civil society casts Black sociality as disruptive and potentially a threat to the closed world of the liberal imaginary.

Black life bears a sociality that is outside and in excess of modernist or liberal understandings of the subject as constitued in a liberal political order. It is this excess that constantly challenges and disrupts the settled order of repression. As Moten writes: 'I bear the hope that blackness bears or is the potential to end the world' (2013, 739). What is at stake is:

> ...what the vast range of black authenticities and black pathologies does. Or, put another way, what is the efficacy of that range of natural-born disorders that have been relegated to what is theorized as the void of blackness or black social life but that might be more properly understood as the fugitive being of "infinite humanity"...
>
> (Moten 2008, 214)

The reenchantment of the human, the excluded and 'fugitive being' of 'infinite humanity' lies in the struggles that work outside and otherwise to the formal political sphere. There is no hope in or for the liberal political order, rather hope underwrites the potentiality carried in the sociality of the excluded and disavowed which thereby bears the hope of this world's undoing. As Moten argues:

> Our aim, even in the face of the brutally imposed difficulties of black life, is cause for celebration. This is not because celebration is supposed to make us feel good or make us feel better, though there would be nothing wrong with that. It is, rather, because the cause for celebration turns out to be the condition of possibility of black thought, which animates the black operations that will produce the absolute overturning, the absolute turning of this motherfucker out. Celebration is the essence of black thought, the animation of black

> operations, which are, in the first instance, our undercommon, underground, submarine sociality.
>
> (Moten 2013, 742)

This alternative ethicopolitical project, underpinned by hope, operates outside and against the repressive closures of liberal political understandings and the liberal subject, and has been subsequently expanded upon in Moten's work with Stefano Harney (2013; 2021). Their well-cited project *The Undercommons* (2013) is clearly set out as a project of open-ended becoming that works otherwise to the politics of representation:

> We aren't responsible for politics. We are the general antagonism to politics looming outside every attempt to politicise, every imposition of self-governance, every sovereign decision and its degraded miniature, every emergent state and home sweet home. We are disruption and consent to disruption. We preserve upheaval. Sent to fulfill by abolishing, to renew by unsettling, to open the enclosure... We cannot represent ourselves. We can't be represented.
>
> (Harney and Moten 2013, 20)

THE INFINITE HUMAN

Hope, enrolled to enable a struggle to hold open what it means to be human against the 'overrepresentation of Man', presupposes the libidinal grounds articulated by Marcuse; the drive to become that life holds always in excess of governing aspirations towards repression and closure. Advocates of hope's utilisation within alternative ethicopolitical projects have forwarded a multitude of grounds beyond and in parallel to Harney and Moten's analysis of how 'blackness operates as the modality of life's constant escape and takes the form, the held and errant pattern of flight' (2013, 51), of open-ended futurity, of the 'infinite humanity' to come. This can be illustrated through a brief engagement with how hope and futurity have been articulated in analogous ways in some critical Queer and Crip framings.

This process of building otherwise worlds on the basis of the exorbitant nature of human desires is radically articulated in the work of José Esteban Muñoz, where the starting point is not so much the affirmation of the (Queer) subject as existing in the present, but the subject's need to negate the world, to become otherwise. Muñoz opens his classic text, *Cruising Utopia* with the assertion: 'Queerness is not yet here. Queerness is an ideality. Put another way, we are not yet queer' (2019, 1). Hope thus enables the placing of a very different, and always incomplete, subject at the centre of ethicopolitical claims. Queerness is then not an identity, something to be affirmed as it exists in the present, but a desire to become otherwise: 'Queerness is essentially about the rejection of a here and now and an insistence on potentiality or concrete possibility for another world' (Muñoz 2019, 1).

Muñoz's project powerfully utilises hope to clearly articulate a struggle to keep open the possibilities for otherwise worlds: 'These performances are thus outposts of an actually existing queer future existing in the present' (2019, 56). The key point is the tapping into the power of life, of desire: 'This desire does not lead to practical politics or even a critical practice, because pragmatism has only ever failed us' (2019, 121). It is the affirmative performative, creative, affective, additive aspects of minoritarian practice that perform 'a negative function, which is the work of critique' (2019, 125). As Muñoz writes:

> Here we come to understand emancipation as freedom from historical forces that dull or diminish our sense of world... those blockages that disallow our arrival at an actual sense of the world, which is the world as a plurality of senses.
>
> (Muñoz 2019, 204)

The libidinal life-principle that enables hope to drive this alternative ethicopolitical project is clear and is expressed in the desire for openness and collaboration, seeking to remove or work otherwise to the 'blockages' of 'historical forces'. Thus, '[q]ueerness's ecstatic and horizontal temporality is a path and a movement to a greater openness to the world' (2019, 25); 'queerness in its utopian connotations promises a human that is not yet here' (Muñoz 2019, 25–26).

The articulation of the human that is 'not yet here' or of 'new genres of the human' (Wynter 2003), is one that is dependent upon enabling the libidinal, life-driven desires for otherness to disrupt and to problematise imaginaries of closure. Hope underpins this critical mode of being, of practice geared towards opening up and problematising constructions of the modernist human (both individually and collectively constructed) which see the human project as one that is finalised, that is already complete. As Carrie Sandahl puts it, from a disability/Crip theory perspective: 'Cripping [exposes] the arbitrary delineation between normal and defective and the negative social ramifications of attempts to homogenize humanity' (cited in McRuer 2006, 139). This process of problematisation seeks to deconstruct, to hold open categories and assumptions of the subject.

This struggle to hold open may be read as the collective construction of spaces where it is possible to imagine identifications beyond and across identity boundaries. In the work of Robert McRuer, one of the founding scholars of queer disability studies, this holding open aligns with the work of Wynter, Muñoz and others in drawing upon the libidinal desires that are repressed and marginalised. For example, in the construction of space otherwise, 'outside of that privatized space, disability activists… continue to shape fluid and critical identities and creative, radically democratic ways of relating that are neither predictable in advance nor containable within straight ideologies of domesticity' (2006, 102). This experience of struggle is read as transformative and as revealing otherwise worlds as possible within *this* world: 'The queercrip consciousness that emerged... made a return to their former existence—able-bodied, closeted, private, privatized—less imaginable and undesirable' (2006, 103). McRuer also stresses the open-ended nature of a crip theoretical approach, one that argues for 'the difficult but necessary work of continually resisting a pedagogy focused on finished products' (2006, 158); 'projects of resisting closure or containment, and accessing other possibilities, are queer/crip projects' (2006, 159).

The project of opening up and of problematising political identity claims is not a matter of purely empirical differences; of attempting to expand the list of distinct and intersecting perspectives or locations from which critique and struggle can be waged. The aspiration is not a universalising one 'that leaves no form of identity behind' (Bérubé 2006, viii) but rather that of problematising or destabilising discourses of identity that seek closures rather than open-ended processes of becoming. McRuer draws upon Donna Haraway to argue that rather than striving for closure, completeness or for wholeness, 'permanently partial identities' should be the goal (2006, 159). It is for this reason that work in critical Black, Queer, and Crip studies often directly articulates hope within the ethicopolitical positionality of a less-than-whole subject: a subject always necessarily open and in process, never final or closed.

CONCLUSION

This chapter analysed how hope has underpinned alternative ethicopolitical approaches that struggle to hold open alternative futures. This praxis is one that is very much human-centred, with a concern to overcome the alienated condition of this world. However, these approaches were not oriented around a liberal or modernist struggle for state-based institutions or state-based rights. Hope's utilisation is probably at its most radical in this desire to reenchant the human as the possessor of a libidinal life force which exists prior to and in excess of governmental attempts to contain and repress it. Hope's enrolment in struggles to reenchant the human beyond the fixities and constraints of the modernist liberal order has been crucial for critical traditions marginalised or excluded from formal and institutionalised modes of the political. This has been highlighted here, in the analytical engagement with those working in the fields of autonomous Marxism, Black, Queer and Crip fields of struggle. Libidinal drives, the life force of the human, are held to have pre-existed regimes of repression and control, and always to be in excess of regimes of regulation and representation. In articulating these drives and desires, critical activists and theorists necessarily drew upon hope to offer an alternative ground for futural possibility in the face of the exclusionary closures of mainstream and radical political movements.

NOTES

1 This shift towards separation and imaginaries of 'incommunicability' is in some ways counter-intuitive, in that, at the level of cultural, social, economic and, importantly, environmental interaction, it is no longer straightforward to maintain essentialising views of communities imagined as autonomous from external structural influences (Chibber 2013; Sartori 2014; see also Chandler and Reid 2019).

2 Negentropy, refers to the power of becoming, of creative differentiation, which operates against the second law of thermodynamics which states that entropy will tend to increase across time as all modes of differentiated being come to an end (see Weiner 1973).

3 As Marcuse writes:

> ... intensified progress seems to be bound up with intensified unfreedom. Throughout the world of industrial civilization, the domination of man by man is growing in scope and efficiency. Nor does this trend appear as an incidental,

> transitory regression on the road to progress. Concentration camps, mass exterminations, world wars and atom bombs are no "relapse into barbarism," but the unrepressed implementation of the achievements of modern science, technology, and domination.
>
> (1987, 4)

4 This is captured well in Mark Featherstone's analysis, that Negri suggests 'that the productivity of the multitude might eventually overcode the capital control system. Thus, virtuality, or hope, becomes actuality, or practice, and we witness the occurrence of praxis: postmodern communism' (2002, 378).

2

FREEDOM DREAMS

INTRODUCTION

In the first chapter, hope informed ethicopolitical practices focused upon understandings of the human as a libidinal subject. These approaches were worked through in discussion with and against the arguments first developed by Sigmund Freud by critical theorists of the Frankfurt School. In this chapter, the focus is upon a similar but different path through which hope underpins practices of processual becoming, grounded upon the importance of the aesthetic realm of human understanding and imagination. In this framing, it is the Kantian aesthetic which articulates hope via a process of 'liberating the imagination' or 'freeing the mind'. Theorists linked to the Frankfurt School of critical theory were also some of the central interlocutors for this mode of engaging hope as enabling, which has also been crucial for work across the critical tradition.

The first section of this chapter analyses how contemporary theorists draw upon the Kantian understanding of the aesthetic and the sublime, including the important contribution of Jacques Rancière, in centring the role of techniques of 'encounter' and 'seeing', and the 'cosmotechnics' of Yu Hui. The second section engages with probably the most important legacy of Kantian critique, the Black radical tradition, focusing on the 'Black Marxism' of Cedric Robinson, Ruth Wilson Gilmore's work on 'abolition' and Marquis Bey's 'Trans Black

DOI: 10.4324/9781003632719-4

Feminism'. The third section analyses in a little more depth what might be at stake in processual approaches that enrol hope into these ethicopolitical projects – the transformation of the liberal grammar of 'rights', 'freedom', 'abolition' and 'emancipation' – through a discussion of Neil Roberts' concept of 'marronage' and Michi Saagiig Nishnaabeg scholar, Leanne Betsamosake Simpson's conception of 'grounded normativity'.

THE KANTIAN AESTHETIC

From Kant onwards, the critical tradition has understood the human to be both a political and an aesthetic subject. Aesthetic capacities were essential to the modern, or liberal, human as a transformative subject, as reasoning was always contingent and socially mediated. 'Knowledge of objects was, thus, not seen as being structured primarily by their a priori existence, but by the nature of our perception of them' (Bleiker 2001, 513). In fact, it could be argued that the essence of the liberal subject, what makes the human distinct from the non-human, can be better grasped as an aesthetic divide rather than as a divide shaped primarily by the capacities for some 'objective' reason (Jackson 2016; Bradley 2023; Lloyd 2019). This was an aesthetic divide because judgement, decision-making, self-governance, or self-making, depended upon a capacity for distance, for abstraction, from the world as it appears.

Kant's aesthetic training of the subject in the appreciation of beauty is one example of an approach to beauty as something that cannot be rationally grasped as a phenomenon but only experienced 'as if' it was in the world (Hui 2021, 197). This experience of beauty, according to Kant, arises from an attunement of the two representational powers, understanding and imagination (Brigstocke and Noorani 2016, 2). Thus, aesthetic judgement is, for Kant, always already built into the process of human cognition. The human as subject necessarily brings the future into the present, transcendentally aware of a 'sublime' beyond the world of appearances.

David Lloyd (2019, 47–61) usefully engages in an analysis of the centrality of the aesthetic to Kant's understanding of the human as a universal autonomous subject in contrast to the 'physiological' logic of aesthetics articulated by Burke. For Kant, the key to the 'civilising' process is the capacity of the subject to break from being bound to the immediacy of appearances, from the power of the object. Thus, in Kant's Third Critique (*The Critique of the Power of Judgement*, 2002), the properties that are properly aesthetic – beauty and sublimity – are located not in the object itself but rather in the cultivation of aesthetic capacities, the 'disposition' of the subject itself for reflection and judgement (Lloyd 2019, 48–49). Beauty, as with the sublime, is in the eye of the beholder, provided that they have developed the capacities to be self-determining rather than being trapped in a world of 'affectability' and the dangerous immediacy of the senses (Lloyd 2019, 52; see also Silva 2007).[1]

For Kant, freeing the mind from the constraints of immediacy created the foundation of a liberal ontology, a shared 'common sense', where the subject mediated their thoughts and feelings via the assumption of representing a collective, shared, perspective. Thus, abstraction from natural ties and entanglements enabled the universal subject to emerge beyond the immediacy of the particular. It is this aesthetic aspect which is key to the liberal or modern subject as self-determining rather than being determined by external forces. The subject is able to emerge as 'free' in so far as they can represent the object in a detached way, rather than be determined by the object itself. This is the power of self-determination at the heart of what could be called the 'aesthetic' mode of enrolling hope for the reenchantment of the human. In this way, hope informs an emancipatory practice which seeks to free the human subject through making a break from the hold of the object, the hold of appearances, the hold of immediacy.

Hope underpins an agent- or subject-centred capacity of thinking beyond or at the limits of immediate appearances and is therefore central to the construction of a modern ontology of subject and world and the telos of forward moving time, as the imagined movement of the abstract transcendent human subject itself. However, for Kant, the subject had no direct experiential knowledge of reality as such. The gap between experiential, representational, knowledge and reality was assumed to be of little practical importance as the world beyond human sensibility was inaccessible but necessarily assumed to be 'providential', aligned to human aspirations. This was to change with the growing disillusionment with modernist assumptions after the First World War and even more so through the disasters of the early- and mid-20th century (Benhabib 1990, 1438). The gap – between the abstract reasoning, so praised by Kant, and the world in reality – began to appear as much more problematic. Thus, the focus upon the aesthetic shifted to the need for a break from dominant imaginaries and modes of thought, rather than just making a break from the immediacy of the appearances, of the givenness, of the world.

It is these shifts which enable contemporary aesthetic frameworks to utilise hope in their critiques of Enlightenment 'rationalism'. Seyla Benhabib argues that the critical tradition of aesthetics is at the heart of the work of the Frankfurt School:

> For Adorno and Horkheimer, the space occupied by the aesthetic is defined by the parameters of the critique of discursive logic. The aesthetic emerges as the only mode of expression that can challenge the compulsive drive of Western reason to comprehend the world by making it like itself, by systematizing it, by abstracting from it, or in Max Weber's terms, by "rationalizing" it. The aesthetic intimates a new mode of being, a new mode of relating to nature and to otherness in general.
> (Benhabib 1990, 1443)

It was the Frankfurt School that developed an approach to aesthetics as an ethical and political project oriented towards negating the identitarian logic of modernist thought, enabling the otherness that was repressed to come to the fore. Thus, the work of critical aesthetics is often considered to be one that privileges difference and alterity. As Laura Shepherd writes: 'An aesthetic sensibility recognises the futility of efforts to capture the world *as it really is*, understanding that "[a]ny form of representation is inevitably a process of interpretation and abstraction"' (2017, 215, italics in original). Rather than a representative understanding of the world as given, Roland Bleiker argues:

> An aesthetic approach, by contrast, assumes that there is always a gap between a form of representation and what is represented therewith. Rather than ignoring or seeking to narrow this gap, as mimetic approaches do, aesthetic insight recognises that the inevitable difference between the represented and its representation is the very location of politics.
>
> (Bleiker 2001, 510)

This critical gap between the way the world appears to thought and the world that lies behind these constructed appearances is the location of a different type of politics, one in which hope informs a radical and critical practice. In this way, hope is central in the construction of worlds operating outside or working against hegemonic constraints and understandings, drawing critical theorists, seeking to move beyond and to challenge dominant modes of representation, towards marginal lifestyles, held to be able to construct alternative modes of subjectivity (see Žižek 2008, xxiv). These marginal lifestyles are often understood to be resistant to homogenising repressive norms and values and therefore as capable of expressing aesthetic impulses that point beyond modernity's alienating social order (Marcuse 1987; Schoolman 1976).

A key theorist renowned for developing critical thought in relation to this aesthetic 'gap' is Jacques Rancière. Rancière challenged Kant's abstract assumptions of a universal transcendental subject which developed a timeless set of practices informed by hope, of attuning to the sublime beyond the world of rationalisation. He did this through constructing aesthetic practice as not just a way of grasping the world but as a way of understanding ways of grasping the world. Hope, expressed through the desire to see or sense beyond the given, in this way, becomes a contested practice and a subject of political contestation itself (Jackson 2016, 10). Thus, in essence, for Rancière, politics is the process of putting in question hegemonic modes of being as particular 'partitions of the perceptible' (Rancière 1999) or 'distributions of the sensible' (Rancière 2024).

Rancière therefore understood aesthetics to describe regimes in which what is capable of being said, seen or sensed and what is excluded are understood to autonomously come into being as expressions of modes of communal existence (Rancière 2024, 19). This mode of existence is then itself subject to question, to disruption, by alternative 'distributions of the sensible' in which aesthetic claims and political claims are inseparable (1999, 59). In this way, communal and political life becomes an 'aesthetico-political field of possibility' (Rockhill 2024, xvi). Still working within the Kantian tradition (Frost 2010), Rancière seeks to place aesthetics in a central role in the development of the subject, operating below the level of consciousness but also available to shape and be shaped by contestatory practices:

> If the reader is fond of analogy, aesthetics can be understood in a Kantian sense... as the system of a priori forms determining what presents itself to sense experience. It is a delimitation of spaces and times, of the visible and the invisible, of speech and noise, that simultaneously determines the place and the stakes of politics as a form of experience.
>
> (Rancière 2024, 8)

In fine, Rancière draws out a distinction between two modes of the avant-garde which can be understood to operate across the political and aesthetic fields, involving 'two different ideas of political subjectivity' (2024, 25). The first mode is that of the 'archi-political', the strategic rationalist mode of the revolutionary party seeking to seize state power and pursue a programme of transcendent goals. The second is that of the 'meta-political', 'the idea of the potentiality inherent in the sensible modes of experience that anticipate a community to come'; this is the aesthetic practice underpinned by hope (Rancière 2024). Aesthetics is necessarily grounded in community practices; aesthetic practice informed by hope is thereby as much a material as an ideational one. For Rancière:

> Thus, it is not a matter of claiming that 'History' is only made up of stories that we tell ourselves, but simply that the 'logic of stories' and the ability to act as historical agents go together. Politics and art, like forms of knowledge, construct 'fictions', that is to say *material* rearrangements of signs and images, relationships between what is seen and what is said, between what is done and what can be done.
>
> (Rancière 2024, 35)

In this way, the human as subject is shaped through a 'meta-political' struggle over the distribution of the sensible rather than struggles constrained within the formal political sphere. The turn towards aesthetics takes the form of the 'meta', a way of articulating politics more broadly, operating beyond and outside the narrow framework of formal political contestation. As Bleiker argues:

> Direct aesthetic encounters with the political can contribute to a more inclusive and just world order, for they challenge our very notion of common sense by allowing us to see what may be obvious but has not been noted before.
>
> (Bleiker 2001, 526)

However, the problem is how to engage with these aesthetic sensibilities, that operate below the level of conscious acceptance of the world as given. For Bleiker, for example:

> To think of the unthinkable, however, is not as far-fetched as it seems at first sight. Most people experience moments when the language available to them is not adequately suited to express exactly what they feel… What is needed is a more fundamental aesthetic encounter.
>
> (Bleiker 2001, 531)

It is through this 'encounter', that theorists argue subjectivities can be challenged and potentially shifted. Laura Shepherd pursues this line of argument to highlight the encounter with otherness as a necessary opening to thinking and becoming otherwise (2017). Hope informs understandings of the internal process of (re) thinking that the encounter can set into motion. This makes practices informed by hope necessarily relational ones; there would merely be idle speculation if there was no encounter that was sufficient to shake, to destabilise, existing modes of perceiving the world.

The way that hope is put to work is thus very different to the work of the imagination, if this is understood to presuppose a passive relation to the world of the present, where the task might be 'to imagine more hopefully; to imagine better' (Hawkins 2025, 2). It is the 'encounter' with some form of 'otherness', with alterity, that produces a disjuncture, enabling an opening against the closures of modernist thought. Hope thereby informs not merely a set of practices which disturb or unsettle the limits of what can be thought or imagined but also facilitates a training in being in the world (Jackson 2016, 10). Hope, in this way, underpins the art, the poetics, the practice, of holding open alternative futures. Not according to a definitive plan but according to the 'authentic' nature of the subject's true being, which emerges through the encounter, through the disruption or destabilisation that puts in question the existing mode of perception.

Yuk Hui's *Art and Cosmotechnics* (2021) provides a very clear contemporary example of how relational encounters can be approached as a critical training in aesthetics as a practice informed by hope. In doing so, he draws upon and reworks a number of aesthetic traditions from Greek tragedy, German idealism and Chinese philosophy. The importance of aesthetics, as stated above, is for the training of a sensibility towards a beyond of what is immediately available to experience (Hui 2021, 29). The capabilities that Hui looks to develop are intuitive rather than rationalist; capacities for resonating beyond the given of appearances, refusing 'to accept the phenomenal world as it is' (Hui 2021, 276). Of course, aesthetic practices and training can take many forms, from expressionist art to Buddhist approaches to gardening. The point is that intimations of the ungraspable outside work to undermine or to destabilise the idea of a coherent subject/world relation. This process of unmaking or unlearning thereby decentres rather than affirming the subject, offering a 'radical opening to the unknown' (Hui 2021, 48). However, as stated, it is important that speculation is not just arbitrary but needs to be grounded in cultural and subjective sensitivities of time and space. This training in sensibility, Hui calls 'cosmotechnics'.

Hui makes the point that, in this way, the encounter with the unknown is experienced 'not as mystery, but as openness' (2021, 198). An aesthetic training is thereby not about painting what is seen, the literal or figurative, but going beyond what is perceptible or sensible (Hui 2021, 200). While Kant wished to limit speculative reasoning, Chinese philosophy, according to Hui, precisely, wishes to cultivate it (Hui 2021, 201). 'The unknown has to be recursively rationalized through the known' (243). Here, the links between Hui's work and other contemporary speculative approaches to aesthetics, such as new materialism, speculative realism, and Object-Oriented

Ontology, are clear in their articulations of an ethical training in enablement. Hui takes inspiration from abstract artist Wassily Kandinsky's aesthetic gaze (Hui 2021, 117) which enables cigarette butts, buttons and pieces of bark and a calendar page, to bring 'dead' objects to life. This passage directly parallel's American political theorist Jane Bennett's similar aesthetic desire in *Vibrant Matter* (2010, 4) where the 'glove, pollen, rat, cap [and] stick' stuck in a storm drain 'shimmied back and forth' no longer inert but calling, 'provoking affects' with their 'thing power'. This is an aesthetic gaze which seeks to go beyond the literal, beyond representation, to intuit a beyond.[2]

This approach to aesthetic practice, informed by hope, is at the heart of a range of contemporary critical approaches that focus upon moving beyond the world of human exceptionalism and the human/nature divide to develop 'greener' and more 'ecological' sensibilities (Bennett 2010, xiv; 10). For speculative thinkers, this can be done by working on our own powers of becoming affected, our experiential being in the world, cultivating openness to alterity. As Bennett states: 'The ethical task at hand here is to cultivate the ability to discern nonhuman vitality, to become perceptually open to it' through techniques of 'training oneself' (2010, 14). Hope informs this mode of speculative critique, which is at the centre of the work of political theorists William Connolly (2011; 2013) and Jairus Grove (2019). Grove, in rejecting the 'crypto-providence' of Kant (2019, 234), asserts that hope lies in understandings of complexity and creativity that Connolly argues are 'non-providential' (2019, 239). Hope, for Grove and for Connolly (as for Bennett), informs a speculative practice oriented towards the development of the subject making a break from the world of actualised appearance.

Thus, 'Connolly's political theorist as seer... attempts to peer into the future, but the seer looks for incipient possibilities, not catastrophic certainties' (Grove 2019, 264).

Drawing on Deleuze, Connolly argues for a pre-emptive generosity and openness to the inaccessible beyond, imagining 'a seer dwelling within a nest of partly formed potentialities jostling against and upon each other during a forking moment, with no potentiality settled enough to be foreseen with certainty' (Connolly 2011, 158). Rather than focusing on saving the world as it exists in appearance, speculative political theory, 'the politics of becoming', works with hope and 'suggests an enhanced attentiveness to materiality and the chaos of becoming' (Grove 2019, 269). As Connolly writes, 'A seer by definition lives at the edge of power and events' (2011, 159) living not at the centre of a modernist imaginary, but 'dwelling sensitively' (2011, 165), on the edge, with incipient hope in the beyond.

Thus, aesthetics (or the art of cosmotechnics, in the terminology of Hui) could be seen as the 'epistemology of the non-rational' (Hui 2021, 123) or 'the epistemology of the unknown' (Hui 2021, 254), 'beyond phenomenal truth' (Hui 2021, 123). In this way, opening to alterity, even if this alterity is ungraspable or not fully knowable, seeks neither to affirm the being of the world nor the subject (165). The other, the outside, the unknowable, is the basis for rethinking 'the distribution of the sensible', as a process of destabilisation and disruption (Hui 2015). This unknown is a barrier to rationalist forms of appropriation but provides a training for sensitivities, for attunement, for resonance, enabling capacities for responsivity, for reacting to contingency and spontaneity, and thereby holds open alternative futures in the face of the multiple closures of broken worlds (2021, 173–174). Thus, perhaps counterintuitively, the emphasis on the negative, on non-relation and the unknowable, on the project of the undoing or the unmaking of the subject, is one of adaptive growth and development (see also Rei Terada's analysis of Hegel and negation in *Metaracial*, 2023). This 'development' is not so much in the knowledge and skills required to act upon a knowable external world but in enabling the subject's becoming through the use of the external world as a foil to 'liberate' or 'emancipate' the subject from its own perceptual limitations (Žižek 1993).

The subject-centred perspective, whereby hope underwrites these aesthetic projects of critique, is an important aspect of contemporary ethicopolitical work that seeks to reenchant the human subject. If the human is to bear the weight of constructing alternative futures to come, then it must be not only exorbitant to regimes of representation and repression, but this exorbitance must also be the grounds for its own transformation as an ethicopolitical actor. It is aesthetic work on the self that is then key to hope's enrolment in modes of disruptive, problematising and critical practice. As Mark Jackson argues:

> The effort is not to wallow in passivity, but the opposite: to impel acting toward possibility through self-criticality. As such, attunement via the aesthetic becomes a means to capture not the impossibility of representation, but the abyssal, nonexhaustiveness of political subjects... human and nonhuman... and their always already excessive capacities to become otherwise through aesthetic experience and practice.
>
> (Jackson 2016, 15)

THE BLACK RADICAL TRADITION

The capacity to become otherwise through aesthetic experience and practice in which the subject's agency and autonomous drive comes to the fore has been central to a 'Black radical tradition' or 'Black radical imagination'.[3] This is articulated well by Cedric Robinson, who introduced the concept of the Black radical tradition in his *Black Marxism* (2000 [1983]). To highlight the methodological approach, throughout his *An Anthropology of Marxism* (2019 [2001]), a process ontology is clearly positioned against an emphasis on an economic determinist analysis of the world. In opposition to the determinism of Marxists, with their so-called 'objective conditions', Robinson places an emphasis on the importance of individual agency, upon consciousness, upon the mind and the power of the imagination. He argues that for Lenin, Marx and Engels: 'It is not the consciousness of men that determines their existence, but their existence that determines their consciousness' (2019, 3).[4] Thus, 'historical determinism' is held to have reduced social actors, even the 'proletariat' themselves,[5] to playing a bit part in a drama led and informed by elite bourgeois intellectuals who were to interpret the 'objective' conditions and enlighten the masses when the time was right.

Key to Robinson's integration of hope into radical aesthetic practices is the rejection of the modernist separation between subject and object, that made the world available as a ground for a linear and universal 'science' of politics, which continued the bourgeois imaginary of control, mastery and instrumentalisation (Robinson 2019, 59; 109).[6] Both the world and the subject become reworked in processual terms. However, the logical implications of this shift are that the world is less available for causal explanations and analysis. This can be traced in Robinson's own work, for example, in the shift away from the focus on the struggle against 'racial capitalism' in 1983s *Black Marxism*, the foundational text for establishing the Black radical tradition. In his later manuscript, *An Anthropology of Marxism* (2019 [2001]), resistance to power and oppression, capitalism and class struggle are much less central (see Robinson et al 2022, also Gordon 2019, 128, n.8).

Understanding hope as enabling practices of holding open alternative futures in broken worlds, articulated as processes of continual becoming, easily flattens any distinction between resisting regimes of domination and the construction of new modes of being. This is because the political and ethical struggle is not mediated through a process of formal politics or through state institutions.

Robin Kelley argues in *Freedom Dreams* that the Black radical imagination is not 'utopian, idealist, and romantic' (2022, 7); the 'effort to see the future in the present' is based not on scientific but rather 'poetic knowledge' (2022, 9). In refusing what *is* and focusing on potentiality, hope informs an ethicopolitical alternative which could be understood as both abolitional and creative. As Kelley writes, 'When I use the word "hope," it does not mean wishful thinking or even dreaming... it is not enough to imagine a world without oppression' (2022, xviii). Hope thereby underpins a mode of ethicopolitical agency, a struggle that shares 'a vision of a future grounded in love, mutual care, cooperative economies, transformative justice, and abolition' (2022, xxi). This ethicopolitical project centres the importance of hope in making aesthetics, ethics and politics indistinguishable and refusing the hegemonic demands – for 'realism', for pragmatism and acceptance – that seek to maintain or prolong the status quo.

Freedom dreaming is an 'abolitionist framework' that is not about winning or losing state power or 'the resolution of all contradictions and antagonisms but instead offers a path for new ways of living and being together, where every life belongs, is valued, heard, respected, and protected' (Kelley 2022, xxxix). This project requires hope because it is driven by love, by care, and, most importantly, the centring of human faculties beyond rational political calculation and instrumentalisation. It is for this reason that Kelley argues: 'queer and trans liberation means more than visibility or rights, or even the end of capitalism, racism, ableism, violence, and war, but new ways of being free that centre joy and pleasure' (Kelley 2022, xxxiii). Hope informs and enables this ongoing struggle of 'liberation' or 'emancipation' where the open-endedness of the process is key. As Kelley writes: 'Making *revolution* meant remaking ourselves, insisting that the fundamental question facing humanity was how we "grow our souls"' (2022, xvii).

The radical, agential and subject-centred ontology, at the heart of the Black radical tradition, grounds a set of aesthetic, ethical and political practices enabling 'seeing the future in the present'. The goal of negating the world becomes infinitely extended beyond any particular goals or social structures that exist in actuality (Koddenbrock 2014). This is captured well by activist scholar Ruth Wilson Gilmore's long-standing work on abolition. She argues that this is a generic struggle against the 'system's apparently boundless boundary-making', against 'carceral geographies' that need to be met by the struggle for 'abolition geography', a struggle of 'place-making' against 'boundary-making' (Koddenbrock 2014, 231).

This struggle, structured by the Black radical tradition, is 'shaped by energetically expectant consciousness of the direction toward unboundedness… inexactly, movement away from partition and exclusion – indeed its inverse' (Gilmore 2017, 237). Thus, the struggle has its own immanent or internal drive that requires conscious organisation and direction. 'Abolition is a totality and it is ontological. It is the context and content of struggle, the site where culture recouples with the political' (Gilmore 2022, 42). Against the 'low flying economism' of the left (2022, 273) who reduce the world to a problem of capitalism, as a prelude to otherwise worlds, Gilmore centres the ongoing work of struggle which is the reworked and rearticulated constant, the 'consciousness-foundation' or 'infrastructure of feeling' that 'underlies our capacity to recognize viscerally (no less than prudently) immanent possibility' (2022, 490).

This processual understanding is highlighted by Liat Ben-Moshe, who conceptualises abolition work as 'dis-epistemology', rejecting readymade prescriptions, definitive knowledge claims and certainties, for reproducing 'carceral logics' of hierarchy and control (2018, 347; see also Raghavan 2024). This understanding is reinforced by Marquis Bey who argues that: 'Abolition is not one spectacularized event but a quotidian working toward eradicating logics as predicates for sociality and relationality' (2022, 22). In this framing, abolition can have no limits 'in service of a radically open claimability and indiscriminate demand', such that 'we cannot simply be "in support" of abolition without sullying ourselves and dissolving, abolishing, the very things abolition stands in contrast to, meaning that we, too, *become* through abolishing the ways we ourselves have been formed' (Bey 2022, 25).

Hope thereby informs critical and aesthetic projects which focus on the mind as the focal point for their liberatory impulse (Lipsitz 2017, 109).[7] The capacity, the desire, for holding open alternative futures and otherwise worlds necessarily pre-exists modernist modes of regulation, capture and repression (Burris 2017, 127). Aesthetic and imaginative capacities to think and dream otherwise are not determined by the material and structural conditions but exist independently and in excess of them. In this way, for the Black radical tradition, it is possible to develop 'the art of living democratically, even under tyrannical regimes, however these regimes are characterized' (Quan 2017, 174, n.7). The barrier that needs to be overcome is one of consciousness rather than a material one: one of 'epistemological investments in political order and a modern ontological commitment to governability' (Quan 2017, 179). As Damien Sojourner notes, 'Western civilization's greatest fear and a core tenet of the Black Radical Tradition – [is] the restructuring of the mind' (2017, 71).

Perhaps one of the clearest articulations of the way that hope underpins the ethicopolitical potential for remaking the subject and holding open the possibilities of the human to come, can be found in the work of Marquis Bey, particularly in their book *Black Trans Feminism* (2022), where 'fugitive' hope is addressed at length. Bey makes the 'paraontological' point, 'that black trans feminism is not *about* black trans women' (2022, 32); it is not about any form of identity politics and thereby any form of intersectionality. For Bey, there can be no fixed relation between a particular type of body or identity and any particular political outlook or phenomenological experience. If hope is to inform a project of open-ended critical futurity, then reductive categories and differentiations have to be seen as 'at base, violences structured and created by forces of hegemony': 'To be understood as a categorically black or trans or woman is, fundamentally, an identity imposed—a "given ontology"—that, ultimately... must be discarded because of its link to being forged in the cauldron of an originary violence' (Bey 2022, 10).

The connection is clear between projects of re/un/making subject identities (genres of the human) and holding open alternative futures against the closures of the modernist imagination:

> To inhabit the world as unfixed requires one to let go profoundly. But this profound letting go is with respect to a profound gaining of something else that might allow us to do things differently. The present conditions must undergo an immense detachment; we must detach, unfix, from such conditions if we are to engender something other than this. It is untenable to stick with what we have now, what exists now, if we heed that a radical end of the world requires a radical *end* of *this* world and its signatories. The other world that is here and now, an other world that harbors otherwise states of becoming and a "you beyond you"...
>
> (Bey 2022, 12)

The open-ended project of critical praxis, informed by hope, is one that is more concerned with the subject's capacity for reimagining the world in open-ended ways than with the materiality of the world in itself (2022, 115). In fact, Bey states that: 'Readers may have begun to notice something that could be seen as troubling—namely, the overlooking of structural barriers' (2022, 14). The critical ethicopolitical claim of a processual alternative, depends upon thinking outside these 'structural barriers': 'An outside to the structures must be imagined if there is any chance in negating their sovereignty' (2022, 14). For Bey, this is precisely where blackness, transness and feminism come in: 'They outlast the identities often sutured to them because, as engendering fugitive forces, they precede and exceed their capture in these identities' (Bey 2022).

Alternative modes of ethicopolitical activity, underpinned by hope, thus articulate abolition in terms that apply less to the structured oppressions and exclusions of the external world than to the identity of the subject itself, which requires 'ungendering', 'a refusal of an "identity," and furthermore of an ontological ungrounding' (2022, 67). Bey's radical agenda is the refusal of the imposed categories of identity and meaning: 'we must let go, yes, of the things that we hold so dearly—of our "race," of our "gender," of our "humanity"—because those things were imposed, violently, nonconsensually, and in fact impede our ability to come together' (2022, 137). More importantly, what is needed 'is a radical delinking of who we think we are from who we believe we can be... to extricate ourselves from humanity... to unbecome humans' (Bey 2022).

What is crucial to the argument being made in this chapter is that hope's enrolment can be seen to become increasingly problematic in these ethicopolitical articulations. This is because the focus on the remaking of the subject risks leaving the world as it is, not just unquestioned but, in fact, affirmed in its reality 'beyond' the 'carceral' categories of the modernist repressive order. This problem comes to the fore in Bey's Kantian belief that another world must be there 'for us', otherwise why would we desire its coming into being? Why would we always, already, have a desire to become otherwise? Otherwise, why would hope exist as an internal resource, driving us beyond what we have? Otherwise, why would we be human?

> There must be a preconditioning force for engaging in struggle to refuse to let the world remain as such despite its longevity. Different futures are possible; radically altered presents are possible; and, further still, the historical record is mutable... because the world and its constituents are never, and have never been, finalized.
>
> (Bey 2022, 203)

The enrolment of hope as a political praxis, for 'new genres of the human' (Wynter 2003), necessarily continues the Kantian tradition. Hope, in this tradition, as Bey argues, is not 'the belief that all will be fine' but the opposite, that we are compelled to act to hold open alternative futures and to act 'as if' other worlds are possible. If this is the case and we start with these ways in which hope is engaged – to argue that the barrier to human becoming is the internalisation of socially repressive reasoning – then there is no alternative to taking up the politics of 'black trans feminism', the politics of 'fugitive hope', in order to 'escape from fixed rootedness' and thus ground 'a radical opening of possible futurity' in processes of becoming otherwise (2022, 203).

FREEDOM AS A PROCESS OF BECOMING OTHERWISE

In its focus upon processes of openness and becoming, the Black radical tradition, makes a major contribution to the problematisation of the closures and fixity of liberal rights discourse and the broader modernist paradigm of binary categories and positions. In articulating this alternative understanding, the emphasis is placed upon the important role of aesthetics, the imagination, and on psychology, for understanding freedom – the 'metaphysics of freedom' – in processual terms (Roberts 2015, 117). This problematic is perhaps most clearly exemplified in Neil Roberts' work *Freedom as Marronage* (2015), which focuses on the 'process by which people emerge *from* slavery *to* freedom' (2015, 4). Here, 'Marronage fills the discursive conceptual void' (2015, 9) conceptualising agency as a process of becoming, as 'agency within potentiality' (2015, 10). Marronage is a processual 'state of being', neither an individual act of escape or flight nor the creation of a fixed territorial community (2015, 11) but an open-ended process of becoming.

In a liberal ontology of binary cuts and divisions, the subject is either free or unfree, there is no conceptualisation of anything in between. There is no processual becoming in a liberal or modernist conception of political agency. The open-ended approach of abolition moves apposite to liberal understandings of 'negative' or 'positive' freedom, freedom 'from' and freedom 'to' (see discussion in Roberts 2015, 13–15). As Ben-Moshe notes, W.E.B. Du Bois, in *Black Reconstruction* (1998 [1935]) already made the fundamental point that emancipation, the formal abolition of chattel slavery in the United States, was not enough to abolish slavery, but merely rewrote its terms, through the establishment of new institutions (formal and informal) that reproduced racial inequalities (see also Hartman 1997). What might seem to be a realm of freedom to white civil society was a realm of unfreedom from the perspective of those racialised as Black.

It is for this reason that Roberts argues that freedom is a comparative not a closed, absolute or final condition. Drawing upon, former slave, Frederick Douglass' work, he argues that Douglass made a 'conceptual breakthrough' in realising that slavery and freedom should be understood as psychological, mental, conditions as much as material ones (2015, 77). You can be a slave but have the potential to act in ways that resist unfreedoms as much as you can be formally free and mentally enslaved to hegemonic values and understandings. The capacity for freedom can be developed or undeveloped whether you are free or enslaved (Roberts 2015, 77–78). Perhaps even more to the point, from this perspective, as Roberts draws out:

> ...focusing on the agency of slaves shows why adopting a dialectical approach to the relationship between slavery and freedom is a necessary but insufficient criterion for outlining the full contours of freedom. The perspective of slave agency also accentuates why slavery, and not freedom, is the foundational human condition.
>
> (Roberts 2015, 87)

Slavery, repression, is our foundational human condition, but we are not always aware of our unfreedoms. Freedom is an experiential priority for those forced to be (or with the capacities to become) conscious of this repressive condition. 'Marronage' or – for other writers (as discussed above) – 'abolition' then become conceptualisations that enable freedom to be grasped in open-ended and processual terms with no finality or closure. The focus upon freeing consciousness is materially grounded in the encounters of the present. Hope, here, is not enrolled in purely idealist ways; it always informs a 'concrete Utopia' (Bloch 1986, 205), not in terms of goals or aspirations but in the grounding of the agency of the human subject as a capacity exterior to and in excess of existing social and political structures of power. Whereas, for Freud, our unconscious was never available as a guide in the present but always problematic, for discourses informed by hope it can often appear that self-realisation is merely a matter of removing externally imposed limits and restrictions (Eagleton 2017, 102).

It is precisely this utilisation of hope, for the understanding of cognitive openness, at the heart of Robert's conception of marronage, that underpins the work of renowned Michi Saagiig Nishnaabeg scholar, Leanne Betsamosake Simpson. Drawing upon the Black radical tradition by way of Neil Roberts' *Freedom as Marronage* (2015) she describes Indigenous becoming as 'grounded normativity', a form of marronage as a constant act of 'flight out of the structures of settler colonialism and into the processes and relationships of freedom and self-determination' (2017, 17): 'It was a returning, in the present, to myself. It was an unfolding of a different present. It was freedom as a way of being as a constellation of relationship, freedom as world making, freedom as a practice' (2017, 18). Hope, in this way, informs a struggle for autonomy that draws upon pre-existing powers, excessive of and external to, the structures of settler-colonial hegemony.

Simpson argues that for Indigenous resurgence 'our most important work is internal' (2017, 6), stressing the need to 'regenerate the neuropathways for Indigenous living', creating a different future by living differently in the present (2017, 20). In essence, she argues for Indigenous capacity-building, drawing out the inner resources of Indigeneity, through which the individual becomes an 'agent of change', '*presencing the present*' (2017, 20 italics in original). Thus, hope informs a project of holding the future open, calling for 'change from within rather than recognition from the outside' through place-based and relational practices, grounded in community wellbeing (2017, 22) and 'predicated on *deep*, spiritual, emotional, reciprocal, real-world relationships between living beings (2017, 221). In this way, for Indigenous resurgence:

> ...the freedom realized through flight and refusal is the freedom to imagine and create an elsewhere in the here; a present future beyond the imaginative and territorial bounds of colonialism. It is a performance of other worlds, an embodied practice of flight.
>
> (Simpson 2017, 173)

The modality of flight is central to discourses enrolling hope, anticipating 'an elsewhere that is already here, if hidden from view' (2017, 213). Thus, flight is not an escape but a relational grounding. For Simpson, 'flight paths to the future... [are] the opaque Indigenous worlds that Indigenous peoples to varying degrees are already living within' (2017, 213). The future is in Indigenous lives and experiences in the present:

> We don't need a list of demands, because we are the demand. We are the alternative. We are the solution, based on our own nation-based conceptualizations of ourselves. Our bodies and the political orders they house are the demand. Our embodied alternative is the solution.
>
> (Simpson 2017, 237)

Indigenous peoples are their future once they are able to liberate themselves from the repressive constraints of settler colonial modes of thinking and being. The resources for this flight to freedom are internal ones of self-realisation; 'flight' is oriented around 'turning inward', 'using Indigenous processes enacts an Indigenous presence that has the ability to give life to an Indigenous future' (2017, 245).

This framing, of drawing deep on an awareness of potentiality for futures in the present, is not something unique to the Black radical tradition or to critical Indigenous studies and is certainly analogous to more widely articulated activist-oriented approaches, which similarly reject modernist and leftist associations of politics with programmatic manifestos and state power. Perhaps emblematic of this understanding of hope is Rebecca Solnit's well cited and often reissued *Hope in the Dark* (2016), first published in 2004. For Solnit, hope informs assumptions of psychological capacity to 'embrace the unknown and the unknowable' which means that we need to believe 'that what we do matters even though how and when it may matter, who and what it may impact, are not things we can know beforehand' (2016, xii, xxi). Hope thereby enables actors to thrive on ontological uncertainty and imposes a moral duty to act in the world and to realise their agential power.

Hope underpins the generative power that Solnit sees in ordinary people and their struggles of survival and resistance and enables her to argue that the barrier lies in a lack of consciousness of this power: 'often the real goal is to amplify the power and reach of existing alternatives. What we dream of is already present in the world' (2016, xv). Transformations 'begin in the imagination, in hope' and following Ernst Bloch, she argues: 'To hope is to give yourself to the future, and that commitment to the future makes the present inhabitable' (2016, 4). Psychic capacities are central to the transformative project, such that her book is a call to arms: 'I want to start over, with an imagination adequate to the possibilities and the strangeness and the dangers on this earth in this moment' (2016, 5). Hope enables possibility to be grounded in the subject rather than in the world as it appears. She quotes Vaclav Havel, the former Czech president and civil society activist:

> Either we have hope within us or we don't; it is a dimension of the soul; it's not essentially dependent on some particular observation of the world or estimate of the situation. Hope is not prognostication. It is an orientation of the spirit, an orientation of the heart; it transcends the world that is immediately experienced. (Solnit 2016, 11)

Thus, the focus becomes the mind of the subject rather than the materiality, the disastrousness of the world. Solnit writes: 'The revolution that counts is the one that takes place in the imagination... Violence is the power of the state; imagination and nonviolence the power of civil society' (2016, 26–27). Solnit calls this struggle, to hold the future open against the closures of broken worlds, prefigurative politics. It is perhaps useful to quote her understanding of hope as a processual, prefigurative, politics of 'flight':

> Recent strains of activism proceed on the realization that victory is not some absolute state far away... but the flight... The term "politics of prefiguration" has long been used to describe the idea that if you embody what you aspire to, you have already succeeded...

> Activism according to this model, is not only a toolbox to change things but a home in which to take up residence and live according to your beliefs, even it's a temporary and local place, this paradise of participating, this vale where souls get made
>
> (Solnit 2016, 80–81)

This world is not all that there is, but equally no other society or world is the solution either. It is this self-(un)making in the present, the struggle in the here and now to hold open future worlds that matters. Antipolitics, prefigurative politics, the politics of hope as aesthetic practice, are those of flight, of abolition, 'of process not product'. A world that Solnit describes as a 'world in which creation never ends and people participate in the power of being creators, a world whose hopefulness lies in its unfinishedness, its openness to improvisation and participation' (2016, 95). As we have seen, an agent- or process-centred ontology focuses upon the transformative potential of the subject or agent rather than the deterministic role of structures.[8] The world becomes less and less an object for instrumental action and more a speculative field for the experiential becoming of the agential subject.

CONCLUSION

This chapter and the first half of this book have analysed how hope has been drawn upon to inform and underpin ethicopolitical projects of holding open alternative futures in the face of the multiple closures of broken worlds. These approaches and modes of enrolling hope have been distinguished from mainstream approaches which utilise hope in support of the liberal political imaginary of state-based representation and contestation. These ethicopolitical projects have been divided heuristically into two interrelated and cross-cutting approaches. The first, considered in the previous chapter, understood hope to inform projects driven by the enablement of the subject's unconscious libidinal drives and desires (in discussion with and against a Freudian framing of processes of civilisation and repression). The second mode of enrolling hope, considered in this chapter, has focused on how hope has underpinned an aesthetic practice of liberating the mind or the imagination (in discussion with and against a Kantian framing of judgement and representation).

Both these approaches utilise hope for ethicopolitical praxes in ways that are very much shaped by modernist constructions of the political and of the human as political subject. Modernist binary framings carved out the sphere of the political from social and economic relations (the public versus the private sphere), casting the political subject as autonomous, rational and interest-bearing. Futural and processual modes of ethicopolitical praxis, informed by hope, seek to work outside these binary constructions, bringing to the fore aspects and understandings excluded from the liberal ontology and highlighting the centrality of psychological, libidinal and aesthetic drives and imaginaries. However, the projects considered so far share the modernist centring of the human as agential subject with the world as its object, and a temporal imaginary of progress, although recast as the enabling transformation and reenchantment of the human as subject. In both these approaches, the human is very much to the fore and the world is in the background.

When the world does make an appearance in these human-centred approaches, it does so often merely as a foil for the 'flight' of the human subject towards its true and unalienated self. This is the case as much for Michi Saagiig Nishnaabeg scholar, Leanne Betsamosake Simpson, as it is for Rebecca Solnit. Even Solnit's environmental activism places the world as unknowable in order to provide an open infinity for the subject's becoming otherwise. This unknowability makes this framing little different from Kant's aesthetic imaginary where hope is enabling for the civilised subject, able to act 'as if' the world were manageable and open to human control, or the speculative encounter with alterity held to be enabling for the cosmotechnics of Yuk Hui, the interventions of Roland Bleiker and Laura Shepherd, and the work of the 'seer', advocated by William Connolly and Jairus Grove.

These approaches all share a futural telos of human becoming, of reenchantment as processual openness, even if there is a rhetorical focus on 'presencing' the moment and a rejection of ideas of linear progress. Hope thereby informs alternative ethicopolitical modes of practice, within and against modernity, which develop as a response to the closures of *this* world and the perceived constraints to its transformation. These closures were particularly central to those forced to struggle in the context of both exclusion from and disillusionment with modernist promises of democratic inclusion and social justice. The second half of this book examines how hope might be engaged with and put to work differently, underpinning ethicopolitical projects which rather than seeking to reenchant the human at the expense of the world, seek to work the other way: to immerse themselves more in the world, accepting its disastrousness rather than taking 'flight' from it.

NOTES

1 For Edmund Burke, in his *Philosophical Enquiry into the Origin of Our Ideas of the Sublime and the Beautiful* (2015 [1757]), the physical world, i.e., the properties of the object, comes prior to the subject, beauty lies in the object's power over the subject rather than the subjective development of the 'eye of the beholder' and the motive force of the sublime 'lies not in the subject's independence from the object but in his subordination to it' (Lloyd 2019, 55).

2 In this respect, it is possible that the weakness of Bennett's vital materialism is precisely her lack of appreciation of the distinction between the aesthetic approach of problematising assumptions of the world as given and scientific positivist assumptions of an underlying relational reality (Lemke 2021, 151). Thus, for Bennett, there appears to literally be an external materiality that can only be oriented towards through

aesthetic training (see also the critique of Puar (2017, 172 n.67), Hui does not seek to argue this is the case.

3 The Black radical tradition is open to a wide range of interpretations, as David Scott writes, each of the three terms are themselves 'essentially contested concepts' (Scott 2013, 2). I have no intention of making any definitive statement about the Black radical tradition itself, but merely to draw upon the work of a number of authors who claim to be working within it.

4 In the book's footnotes, Robinson repeatedly critiques the early Marx's structuralist understanding that: 'It is not a matter of what this or that proletarian or even the proletariat as a whole *pictures* at present as its goal. It is a matter of *what the proletariat is in actuality*' (Robinson 2019, 132–133, n.35; 151, n.119; 161, n.5).

5 Robinson writes that 'In much of the Marxist imaginary, slaves contributed nothing to revolutionary thought or organization; neither did serfs, peasants, or women from any class or strata' (2019, 15; see also 110; 119).

6 Robinson argues that 'one of the apparent ironies of Marxism' is the rejection of Kant's subject-centred idealism for Hegel's historical materialist understanding of the progress of Western Reason (2019, 72); this understanding is reproduced in his preference for the medieval radicalism of the Jesuits' radical advocacy of a timeless natural law approach to social equality and justice (Robinson 2019, 107; also 115–116).

7 As Robinson states of the Black radical tradition in *Black Marxism*: 'always, its focus was on the structures of the mind. Its epistemology granted supremacy to metaphysics not the material' (2000, 169).

8 The implications of an agent-centred approach, in its move beyond a modern ontology of entities and articulation of agency, can be gleamed from James Der Derian and Alexander Wendt's edited collection, *Quantum International Relations* (2022). Hope, mobilised to inform ethicopolitical practices aspiring to see the future in the present, would seem to work analogously to the quantum imaginary where all that exists is in-potentiality and where every subject is nondetermined or incomplete, always in process, and thereby conceived 'literally [as] "walking wave functions"' (2022, 15; for a critique, see Donald 2018). Here is the world as truly otherwise, as infinite in its plenitude.

PART TWO

SURVIVANCE

3

WORLDING

INTRODUCTION

The second half of this book considers how ethicopolitical practice is informed by hope in ways that more directly reflect the end of confidence in modernist assumptions of progress. The first two modes of enrolling hope, addressed above, relied on different imagined attributes of the human subject: either the repressed libidinal drives and desires or the capacity to make an aesthetic break from hegemonic constraints. The third mode of drawing upon hope puts the emphasis much less on human autonomy from constraint and more on the necessity of new forms of responsibilisation. It is for this reason that hope is deployed in approaches which seek to address problems of sustainability and survivance, not so much within a problematic of social justice but of communal duties in relation to nature and the environment. Rather than the focus upon the individual as 'seer' or making the aesthetic break towards 'freedom' from societal norms, societal barriers are perceived more in terms of the cutting of the human from a deeper set of relational dependencies.

Worlding is a process of understanding world-making as an ethicopolitical practice, which brings material relations to the fore, framing the process as 'becoming-with' others. The roots of this modality of enrolling hope lie in Husserlian phenomenology, particularly as reflected in cybernetic thinking and developed by decolonial

DOI: 10.4324/9781003632719-6

scholars. In this way, hope underpins a process of becoming otherwise which assumes plural forms and a world 'in which many worlds are possible' becomes the goal. A more material, relational, framing of aesthetics as a practice of hope sees modes of being human as not merely, as for Foucault, 'epistemes' at the level of thought, but also at the level, as Sylvia Wynter puts it, of 'regimes of being' (Wynter and Scott 2000, 199). This distinction is captured well in the work of Vanessa Andreotti and others in the 'Gesturing Towards Decolonial Futures' collective, articulated as the difference between 'wording the world' and 'worlding the world' (Mika et al 2020; Susa 2019). In the former framing, the subject is at the centre of the construction of its world, whereas in the latter, 'the world is not *our* construction' (Susa 2019, 196). Here, subject- or agent-centred approaches to autonomy are reworked in radical and relational ways, inverting the subject/world dichotomy.

As analysed above, hope was a marginal critical concern until the exhaustion of the modernist project, when instead of delivering on its promise of progress, modernist framings and assumptions seemed to be closing off futural possibilities. Today, when formal modes of governance appear to have lost their attraction, hope enables alternative modes of political understanding and engagement and appears to be central to contemporary subjectivities. As noted in the Introduction to this book, hope is increasingly enrolled in international policy discourses concerned with individual and community survivance, with community and individual resilience, and with new ways of mitigating crises. Survivance as a concept is about more than merely surviving, it also implicitly calls up understandings of resistance and of critique. Hope has become a policy recommendation through its association with futural processes of open-ended becoming; this is particularly the case when hope is utilised critically to argue for removing barriers to human agency (see, for example, Chipato and Chandler 2024a; 2024b).

Key to contemporary framings of alternative modes of ethicopolitical critique, informed by hope, is the way in which critical or resistant terminology has become mainstreamed in international policy understandings (see, for example, Wagner and Hornidge 2025).

This chapter considers how 'worlding' practices have drawn upon hope, firstly analysing the ways in which hope has been engaged with in decolonial thought, heavily influenced by Humberto Maturana's work in cybernetics. Here, the shift from aesthetics, as a process of liberating the mind or the imagination, to aesthesis as a collective practice of world-making is important. However, the shift, from abstract understandings of the subject to communally grounded frameworks of differentiated becoming, highlights the risk that these framings may inadvertently reinforce tendencies towards essentialising and responsibilising communities. This becomes clearer in analysis of the ways in which international policy-discourses have taken up similar frameworks of processual becoming under the rubric of community and individual resilience. The final section of this chapter focuses on this problematic, considering the problem of ontological ambiguity, whereby alternative ethicopolitical practices, underpinned by hope, appear to be forever caught between, on the one hand, idealised and abstract understandings of human becoming which occlude material constraints, and on the other, emphasising material connections and communities with the danger of essentialising and responsibilising marginalised communities.

PLURIVERSAL DESIGN

While Rancière and the critical tradition assume a universal human as subject and universal framings of the formal sphere of politics and aesthetics as a practice, more contemporary framings have sought to move beyond the Western or Eurocentric roots of the critical turn to aesthetics (Brigstocke and Gassner 2021; Lloyd 2019). As analysed above, for critical modes of enrolling hope into ethicopolitical praxis, the world exists increasingly as a foil for overcoming the limits of the subject's becoming. Thus, hope informs a critical practice which is shaped by a modernist set of universal aspirations enabling the subject to continue to reproduce itself within and against the world as its infinite resource. For the reasons outlined above, this idealist, transcendental, framing of hope as 'freeing the mind' is today increasingly placed in question. As an approach, it is too little aware of the racialising bifurcation baked into the aesthetics enabling the universal human to emerge against the world, let alone seemingly oblivious to the problems of instrumentalising the world as a backdrop to human-centred dreams of grandeur in a time of catastrophic anthropogenic global warming (Latour 2018).

The decolonial approach to aesthetics has perhaps been most shaped by authors such as Boaventura de Sousa Santos, Arturo Escobar and Walter Mignolo. All three have drawn upon relational, autopoietic approaches, which articulate the subject as acquiring freedom through self-making as a communal practice of worlding. Mignolo writes that he first came across the work of Chilean biologist and cybernetician Humberto Maturana's *Biology of Cognition* when it came out in 1970 and that, from then onward, he had continued to follow the work of Maturana and his colleague Francisco Varela (Mignolo 2018b, 361). Escobar has also been influenced by Maturana and Varela's work since the early 1980s (Escobar 2017, xiv). Maturana's work was inspired by the work of the biologist Jakob von Uexküll, which focused upon the autonomy of all living systems which develop in their practical and cognitive relation with other living systems. Maturana developed what is known as second-order cybernetics where systems develop and differentiate in relation to others rather than possessing some inner determinate 'essence' or identity.

Translated into human systems or societies, aesthesis as a process of world-making becomes understood as a material, relational, process of becoming, placing the world at the centre and so working differently to the human-centred and individuated processes of 'liberating the mind'. As Arturo Escobar writes, Western approaches to aesthetics enrolled hope to inform practices but in terms that still stressed theoretical reflection rather than embodied relationality (2017, 98). Hope thereby informs a reflexive practice of holding open alternative futures through worlding otherwise in ways that are held to make a break from the Eurocentric critical tradition. The difference is that hope underpins a practice of world-making, which, in this way, involves more than merely the powers of the mind; more than merely making a break from hegemonic categories of perception.

Worlding is a practice that deploys hope in holding the future open through the processual construction of worlds with other actors and agencies. De Sousa Santos has drawn upon Ernst Bloch's understanding of critical hope to articulate alternative ways of knowing and engaging with the world, in the framework of *Epistemologies of the South* (2014). Escobar has focused upon the field of aesthetics in his *Designs for the Pluriverse* (2017), thinking of aesthetics as 'a tool for reimagining and reconstructing local worlds' (2017, 4). Mignolo has developed the understanding of critical aesthetics to make the distinction between what he conceptualises as colonial 'aestheTics' and decolonial 'aestheSis'. As Mignolo argues, in discussion with Rubén A. Gaztambide-Fernández:

> Decolonial aestheSis refers in general to any and every thinking and doing that is geared toward undoing a particular kind of aesthesis, of senses, that is the sensibility of the colonized subject. What decolonial artists want is not to create beautiful objects, installations, music, multimedia or whatever the possibilities are,

> but to create in order to decolonize sensibilities, to transform colonial aestheTics into decolonial aestheSis. In that regard, aestheTics is the image that reflects in the mirror of imperial/colonial aesthetics in the Kantian tradition. Once you delink, you begin to create a world in which decolonial aestheSis has delinked from aesthetics, which has become aestheTics.
>
> (Gaztambide-Fernández 2014, 201)

The distinction, for Mignolo, is one that is grounded in different 'life worlds' (Mignolo 2018b, 365). Gideon Uzoma Umezurike writes that: 'The phenomenological concern which is most pertinent to the phenomenological dialogue with decolonial transculturality is that of the "life-world"' (2021, 177). The phenomenological approach is fundamentally important in that it provides a different route into thinking about post-Kantian hope, one which directly links to contemporary decolonial approaches to critique. These approaches are phenomenological in that they critically reflect upon the entanglement of ways of being in the world with ways of knowing the world. In bringing pre-cognitive givens into consciousness (Umezurike 2021, 175), it is argued that the 'division of the sensible' of the Western or European aesthetic framing, shaped and limited even the Western approach to the natural sciences (Mignolo 2018b, 370). Thus, for decolonial theorists, there is a fundamental distinction between colonialism and coloniality: 'Coloniality names the underlying logic of all Western European colonialism' (Mignolo 2018b, 372). This underlying logic is a mode of being, a set of aesthetic framings that operate outside or below the level of the sensible but function to partition the world into the seen or counted and the unseen or the uncounted:

> Like Husserl's transcendental consciousness, Sigmund Freud's and Jacques Lacan's unconscious, Karl Marx's surplus value, and Noam Chomsky's deep structures, coloniality names something you do not see that works

> in what you do see. You do not *see* coloniality, but there is no way you cannot *sense* it.
>
> (Mignolo 2018b, 372, italics in original)

As Mignolo argues, the phenomenological approach (originally developed by Husserl, see Husserl 1970) opened up the importance of the Kantian gap between regimes of representation and what was to be represented but was originally developed only to analyse the 'life world' of Eurocentric universality (Mignolo 2018b, 365). The decolonial approach to aesthetics comes from a different set of problematics and experiential life worlds, one where the sense of subjecthood, the sense of identity is much less secured (Mignolo 2018b, 367). Thus: 'modernity/coloniality is a decolonial concept. The compound concept undermines, from the life-world of colonial legacies, one of the basic assumptions of Western cosmology-philosophy: that concepts denote, that there is a one-to-one correlation between words and things' (Mignolo 2018b, 373). The struggle to hold open alternative futures, underpinned by hope, lies then in the ability to break free of the constraints of the modernist/colonial condition, using Indigenous aesthesis 'to heal the colonial wound', to restore communities to their authentic becoming with the world. Mignolo argues:

> ...once you realize that you have also been colonized, that your mind, your body, your senses, your sight, your hearing have been modeled by the colonial matrix of power, that is, by its institutions, languages, music, art, literature, etc. - or what is the same as Western Civilization - you begin to "heal." The process of healing is that of becoming a decolonial subject, or "learning to be."
>
> (Gaztambide-Fernández 2014, 207)

'Learning to be', for Mignolo, requires bringing to the surface the forms of exclusion, erasure and devaluation of colonial modernity, and enunciating an alternative mode of aesthesis, of becoming, one which is in tune with a world that is much more contingent and depends upon relational and more-than-human sensitivities. These 'life-worlds' are differentially shaped, attuned to relational embeddedness rather than a modernist set of subject/object separations. Hope thereby informs life practices which seek to shape worlds otherwise to modernist ones because the approach is not one of the subject's becoming against the world as a speculative backdrop. Decolonial aestheSis starts from the subject's capacities to sense and relate to the world rather than drawing upon the subject's desiring capacities of becoming via the power of thought alone.

For both critical and decolonial approaches, hope lies in the inner capacities of the subject to break from hegemonic framings of what is possible. Agential choice is at the centre of both approaches (Umezurike 2021, 187); however, the otherwise world to be built is not a product of human autonomy understood in modernist terms, of 'freedom' and infinite self-making, but rather the choice of a decolonial relational sensitivity. Mark Jackson writes that the practice of aesthesis, of collective becoming rather than of aesthetic reflection, poses a challenge in that it will 'mean engaging a new semiosis for cognition, one that emerges from more-than-human worlds themselves, and not from reflective judgment—a daunting, but essential, task' (Jackson 2016, 20).

It is the world itself that is enabling for decolonial aesthetics rather than the subject's infinite capacities for becoming. Or, more precisely, the subject's infinite capacities for becoming are expanded from the individual in the 'one-world world' of modernity (Law 2015) to infinite subjects in infinite relational worlds. Worlding as a process is one in which 'life-worlds' proliferate to differentiate the world, multiplying and enhancing potentialities, rather than deadening and reducing the world and its future to one homogenous process. De Sousa Santos describes the turn to aesthetics as enabling a 'sociology of absences', recognising that 'realities are actively produced as nonexistent': the reductionist world of colonial reason makes it essential to develop different practices so that 'reality cannot be reduced to what exists' in a modernist framework (2014, 181). Decolonial approaches thereby seek to enrol hope in a critical mode of practice which works to 'expand the present', not by using the world external to the subject as merely a grounds for speculation but through focusing upon potentialities that exist but are unseen (Chandler 2024a).

In articulating hope within this aesthetic formulation, de Sousa Santos draws upon Frankfurt School theorist Ernst Bloch, particularly his concept of 'Not Yet (*Noch Nicht*)' (2014, 182). This is held to be necessary to break from the modernist binary of All/Nothing and instead to appreciate the world in its relational emergence. The focus upon potentialities that are present, 'the sociology of emergences', enables hope to inform ethicopolitical practice, working at 'the horizon of concrete possibilities', 'amplifying the present' and adding to existing reality (2014, 184). As Walter Mignolo argues, decoloniality as an approach 'is neither a "field of study" nor a "discipline" but a way of being in the world, interrogating the structures of knowledge and of knowing that have thrown us, all of us on the planet, into the world' (Mignolo 2018b, 381). This way of being in the world is an aesthetic practice, or aesthesis, that operates to restore connections and relations in order to amplify being, or presence, making the present a focus of 'constant ethical vigilance', caring for 'the unfolding of possibilities' (Santos 2014, 186).

In this way, it is held to be possible to become-with the world, rather than separately, transforming modernist modes of being in the world, giving being 'a denser, more substantive content than the fleeting instant between the past and the future'. Hope thus enables a practice which can be understood to 'world' very differently, whereby 'life-worlds' are much more literally, and materially, 'worlds'.

It is because these worlds are understood to be autonomous that those within them are also understood to be free: 'These societies/worlds in movement are moments in the exercise of cultural and political autonomy—indeed, of ontological autonomy' (Escobar 2017, 174). Here the aesthetic production, be it a song, a work of art or a video diary, is not the important aspect. The aesthetic product is not what counts but rather the process of producing it. Thus, hope as a practice of worlding the world shifts in emphasis from the subject-centredness of 'freedom dreams', of 'liberating the imagination', to the production of the community as a collective process of shared becoming, shared sensitivities, and care in relation to both human and non-human others.

The logical implication of the turn from aesthetics to aesthesis as practices of 'freedom' and 'autonomy', enabling seeing or sensing beyond the given, is that individuals and communities become designers of themselves in their relational becoming. If this is the case, then it is easy to understand individuals or communities that have difficulty coping with adapting to difficult circumstances as in need of some external assistance. The distinction between contemporary understandings of 'life-worlds' and those in the critical tradition are that the concerns are no longer purely to do with the repression of the human as a Kantian transcendental, world-making, self-making, subject. The human and the world are both recast in an extension of the phenomenological tradition whereby the process of world-making becomes reified as the registration of the subject's capacity to world themselves. This being the case, external assistance increasingly takes the form of aesthetic interventions rather than earlier modes of intervention and enablement, for example, through development or humanitarian assistance. As hope informs ethicopolitical approaches which come to displace political frameworks of understanding, international discourses of problem-solving have increasingly taken an 'aesthetic turn' (see Chipato 2024).

Hope enables the construction of the political subject as processual, one that continually makes and unmakes itself in its becoming within the world. As Neil Roberts notes, this framework, which focuses on the adaptiveness of the individual and the limits of thought rather than material conditions, has much in common with contemporary processual understandings which are taken up in international policy regimes, for example, Nobel Prize winning economist, Amartya Sen's *Development as Freedom* (1999). Sen developed a subject- or agent-centred process ontology to articulate 'freedom as development', putting the subject at the centre of poverty reduction policies, not as a pre-given subject before the world, but as always in the process of 'development' (see Roberts 2015, 198, n.82; see also Chandler 2013). This turn to aesthetics thus frames these ethicopolitical practices, underpinned by hope – practices of open-ended becoming as processes of autonomy and freedom – as solutions to the problems and contingencies communities confront today.

The world comes to the fore in these frameworks, reified as the product of human activity and reflecting the subject's relational and ethical awareness. It is of fundamental importance to note that this shift in contemporary modes of enrolling hope, and the aesthetic critique of representation, is grounded upon the assumption that the world is lively and in excess of our understanding; no longer perceived as a passive or fixed backdrop to politics as a purely human drama (see Serres 1995). The materialisation or 'ontologisation' of the 'life-world' is clear in contemporary work which articulates a decolonial approach along the lines suggested by Mignolo, Escobar and de Sousa Santos. For example, Martineau and Ritskes (2014) argue that while the decolonial emphasis has often been on 'epistemic disobedience' and 'liberating the mind', it is important to locate the work of community resistance and community survival in material struggles of land and place (2014, II). As Jackson writes of the Inuit *katajjait* (throat song):

> The sharing back and forth of resonating breath, touch, rhythm, and expression can be described in part by the category aesthetic, but the aesthesis of the song also exceeds what aesthetics makes possible for meaning. In generating a gathering or worlding of care, *katajjait* also worlds forms of sociality and ethical relation outside the colonizing domains of the aesthetic and the subject that it requires for political recognizability.
>
> (Jackson 2016, 20)

Thus, a decolonial aesthetic practice will be authentic to the community, 'collaborative and multi-voiced', where 'the persistence of Indigeneity in the face of diaspora displacement documents and "gives a lesson to" the possibility of other futures that are not yet imagined' (Cravey and Petit 2018, 361, 363). Here, authenticity is argued to be relational rather than an essentialised attribute: 'Indigenous identities can be fluid and changeable, which presents the possibility for new subjectivities and ways of being in the world' (Cravey and Petit 2018, 365). The skills which enable futures to be kept open through human becoming with the world, rather than against it, are those of resilience. It is the resilient subject which provides the model for contemporary practices informed by hope; this subject requires two qualities: firstly, it must of necessity be vulnerable in order to bring to the surface these inner capacities; and, secondly, it must be adaptive, in order to exhibit or to demonstrate these capacities for becoming otherwise. Hope thereby underpins an ethicopolitical practice of human becoming which depends upon relational groundedness and sensitivities to feedback effects, often seen to be lacking in contemporary Western societies (Kimmerer 2015).

RESILIENCE

The 'life-worlds' imagined by critical theorists, such as Foucault and Rancière, in their turn to aesthetics, were driven by the human as self-making subject, resisting the repressive closures of modern society. The 'life-worlds' underpinned by contemporary forms of hope are very different and take aesthetic inspiration from a much more 'worldly' imaginary; powerfully expressed in the Zapatista slogan that we need a pluriverse, 'a world where many worlds fit'. In this framing, as Adorno argues, authenticity, attunement to otherwise worlds in their multiple becomings, can only be retroactively recognised. It becomes a mystical attribute: 'It turns, as it were, into a racial quality of inwardness, which man either has or does not have—a quality about which nothing further can be stated than that, tautologically, there is mere participation in it' (2003, 108).

Just as 'coloniality' is something that is unseen but, as Mignolo argues above, 'works in what you do see', so hope is put to work via a relational process that depends on capacities that are unseen, inner attributes, only apparent indirectly. Either individuals and societies are attuned to their embedded relationality and thereby assumed to be in harmony or at least able to efficiently adapt to unforeseen events and disturbances or they are still repressed and alienated from their 'life-worlds'. In a world where many worlds fit, some individuals and communities are held to adapt – to world their worlds – better than others, as will be analysed in the next section. The difficulty, of course, is that if the capacity for attunement, for sensing beyond the given distribution of the sensible, is an inner capacity, it can only be seen retroactively. In this way, the capacity to hope, becomes both explanans and explanandum, both the futural solution and the retroactive grounds for explaining the problems of unequally distributed capacities and capabilities.

Thus, in contemporary policy discourses, societal distinctions are seen to be self-made and, the world – in its contingent appearance, its facticity – is understood to register this inner and invisible ontological capacity to hope well, to hold futures open and to create space for adaptative self-making. In which case, as Adorno argues, 'the merely existing world… becomes the highest court of judgement over what should and should not be' (Adorno 2003, 106). For this reason, resilience has come to the fore as a policy concept, as 'relational' understandings and approaches have become mainstreamed in policy circles. Relational approaches seek to move beyond 'equilibrium' solutions, solutions which just throw resources at the problem and assume that life or society can continue as before. In a relational framing, problems and difficulties require adaptation, some form of societal change, to cope with changing climate conditions or other shifts in context. Kevin Grove argues that resilience reconfigures thought and practice on human-environmental relations around a 'designerly aesthetics', a principle at the heart of his book *Resilience* (2018). Resilience as an aesthetic discourse very much requires hope to be put to work in these ways to enable a distinct mode of ethicopolitical and aesthetic practice, seeing the world otherwise, beyond abstract, universalist and reductionist assumptions of modern modes of perception (Steinbock et al 2020).

Resilience, as a design process, is at the heart of the policy frameworks suggested by Escobar's *Designs for the Pluriverse* (2017), articulating the possibilities of design not based on top-down instrumentalised outcomes but on immanent processes of 'autonomous' becoming. As Grove explains:

> Recognizing the aesthetic dimensions of resilience thus brings to light how resilience theory operates through a distinct relationship between truth and control. In a complex "environment," the truth of objects lies in their functionality. And their functionality, in turn,

> hinges on their relations with other objects. Control is no longer a matter of predictive knowledge, but is rather an ongoing process of learning about and managing feedback-driven relations between various entities that make up complex social and ecological systems. Rather than a will to truth that reduces reality to universally-valid objective truths that can be folded into a calculative and predictive rationality, resilience theory mobilizes a *will to design* that strives to reduce reality to functional abstractions that can be re/combined with one another in order to solve contextually-specific problems of social and ecological complexity.
>
> (Grove 2018, 103, italics in original)[1]

The relational autonomy at the heart of resilience as an aesthetic process is one of attunement to feedback effects. The difference between discourses of resilience as a policy field and the critical work of decolonial scholars is that the former often pose community-level responses as in need of external support, as problematic or lacking, while for the latter, community-level responses are often praised for their aesthetic approaches to resilience. Decolonial scholars posit the need for alternative 'distributions of the sensible' as do resilience advocates; however, the question is then often one of translation, of orienting approaches in ways in which local or community-level capacities for relational awareness and for autonomous modes of becoming can be (re)constituted (Grove and Adey 2015). It is this need which Arturo Escobar has sought to address with *Designs for the Pluriverse* (2017) which emphasises the importance of ontological framings of life-world design in order to find new, more authentic, ways of 'being-in-the-world' (2017, x), for 'imagining and reconstructing local worlds' (2017, 4), and 'building community resilience as "a collective design project"'(2017, 145).

At the heart of the discourse of authenticity, central to imaginaries of hope which inform these ethicopolitical practices – seeing beyond the given, of attuning to potentialities of emergence, of sensitising to feedback effects – is the need to enhance community and individual freedom and autonomy (Bosch and Promberger 2020). Therefore, practices underpinned by hope are enabled, and resilience is inculcated, through aesthetic design processes that are held to train individuals and communities in autonomy as a practice of 'designing themselves' (Escobar 2017, 5). However, 'autonomy' here requires reworking in line with a world that is also autonomously worlding itself: 'design, in this sense, does not transform the world. It is part of the world's transforming itself' (Escobar 2017, 56 citing Gatt and Ingold). So, implicitly, it is the human that needs to be 'redesigned' to enable the exercise of 'freedom' and 'autonomy'. For this to work, there must be an assumption of an original or inner 'authenticity' that has been repressed by hegemonic realms of representation:

> ...the goal of the ecological designer is to trigger changes in individual and collective orientations, that is, changes in the horizon that shapes understanding... The transformation we are concerned with is not a technical one, but a continuing evolution of how we understand our surroundings and ourselves—of how we continue *becoming the beings we are.*
>
> (Escobar 2017, 116 italics added)

Autonomy is assumed to be a pre-existing condition, as in Western or modernist liberal ontologies of the autonomous subject, a condition that requires retro activation of new and enabling aesthetic regimes;[2] via the development of practices informed by hope, through which individuals and communities can sense, beyond the given appearances, the 'reality' of *this* world. Escobar refers to this as 'redesigning' or 'reinventing' the human (2017, 118, 143) and the development of new aesthetic sensitivities, using the language of 'emotioning' (Escobar 2017, 216), 'presencing' and 'futuring' (Escobar 2017, 125), to emphasise the embedded and relational potentialities at play in designing with rather than against the world. This involves '"letting go," "letting come," enacting, and embodying the emergent' (Escobar 2017, 126); design as 'revealing' rather than as making (Escobar 2017, 133). While 'cosmotechnics' (as analysed in the last chapter) recognises the cultural differentiation engaged in speculative aesthetics, as a form of enabling the becoming of the differentiated subject, this is very different to the autopoietic imaginaries of decolonial 'life-worlds' where, as Escobar states:

> Latin American conceptions of autonomy are predicated on a radical notion of relationality... Autopoietic entities do not preexist their environments; they are mutually constituted... Autopoiesis names a type of self-creation that is anything but autonomous in the modernist sense; it is not about self-sufficiency.
>
> (Escobar 2017, 171)

Autopoiesis, as a 'type of self-creation', worlding in harmony with what the world requires, as Escobar rightly states, 'is anything but autonomous in the modernist sense'. This is because the inner work required of the subject is that of becoming in line with its relational embeddedness. 'Letting go' and 'letting come' – sensing beyond the given – results in a new form of subordination, such that a struggle to hold open alternative futures, informed by hope, becomes better understood in the register of resilience. Resilience approaches require the subject to be sensitive and attuned, and open in the process of adaptation. Because the capacities required are invisible, internal or immanent, and relational, resilience is only apparent after the fact, after the crisis is over and the subject has either demonstrated its 'authenticity', its effective ability to adapt, or not. As Grove argues: 'designerly critique blends techniques of art and science in ways that allow *becoming-otherwise* to *become useful*. This designerly recalibration of critique means that critique no longer *transgresses*; instead, it *makes transgression useful* for specific problems' (2018, 157, italics in original).

Grove states that: 'This is the point where resilience thinking transforms critique into a mechanism of cybernetic control' (2018, 157). This authenticity of survivance has been critiqued by Adorno: 'Simply to be there becomes the merit of a thing. It is guaranteed in the protection of the double sense of the positive: as something existent, given, and as something worthy of being affirmed' (Adorno 2003, 15). Thus, survivance at the margins becomes an example of hope, illustrating the power of non-modernist or non-liberal alternative cosmologies and understandings, held to demonstrate the powers of 'right living' (2003, 19). As Adorno states:

> The logic of the jargon constantly smuggles in what is limited, finally even situations of material want, under the guise of positivity; and presses for their being eternally instituted at just that moment when, thanks to the state of human achievements, such a limitation no longer needs to exist.
>
> (Adorno 2003, 20)

For Adorno, there is something problematic about the requirement of struggle and suffering to become 'authentic', to become resilient, where there can be plenty of destruction 'together with the blackness of fear, sorrow, and death' (2003, 20), 'But' observes Adorno:

> ...the positive, like a tumbler doll, cannot be kept down. Danger, hazard, risking one's life, and the whole characteristic shudder, are not taken all that seriously. One of the Ur-authentic ones in her time remarked that in the innermost core of Dostoyevsky's hell the light of salvation shone again. She had to swallow the reply that hell was then an awfully short railroad tunnel.
>
> (Adorno 2003, 21)

No matter how dark the times or the struggle, hope underpins a set of ethicopolitical practices of holding open futures, which is grounded upon the assumption that the inner capacities of those who prove themselves to be authentic will enable them to survive and others to do the same. It is this capacity, which is passed down, often in narratives of survivance:

> By means of the magic formula of existence, one disregards society, and the psychology of real individuals which is dependent on that society. Thus one insists on the changing of Man, who in Hegel's sense exists merely in the abstract.
>
> (Adorno 2003, 55)

Hope, in this way, underpins the proliferating policy discourses of resilience and becomes the invisible, intangible mechanism which is the 'cornerstone' of resilience (Andriote 2024).

For the argument of this book, it is important to highlight how hope is essential for these ethicopolitical practices, which in their claims of open-ended encounter, always operate against accepted norms and assumptions. Yet, as Adorno argued so powerfully, this critical struggle to always keep open alternative futures seems a strangely comforting one (Adorno 2003, 22). As already implied, this liminal quality of resilience, of 'authenticity', of hope, informing an infinite process of becoming otherwise, can be understood as 'racial quality' because the difference in coping capacities is given a ground of causal explanation. Adorno states that an ontic condition – the appearance – of surviving well or badly in a given context, is then 'ontologised' – taken as the explanation for the contingent and relational capacities. Why some communities might succeed while others are less successful is then put down to inner qualities and capacities which only appear in a particular crisis.

This can be understood as 'racial' as inequalities, as they appear in the world, are no longer seen as sociohistorical products but rather as the external expression of the unseen characteristics of those individuals and communities. Race always involved more than the superficial appearances of skin colour; epidermal and other characteristics were seen as markers for invisible, ontological ones (Silva 2007; Lloyd 2019). Inequality was therefore naturalised, seen as an attribute of different peoples and societies themselves, rather than a product of social and historical relations. Therefore, as Adorno states, 'the mere appearances' of the world are held to reflect these inner and invisible capacities to hope or to become resilient. Hope is put to work then in problematic ways when it is the central underpinning for policy discourses which seek to point to invisible, virtual or immanent capacities and drives, held to be key to alternative futures and otherwise worlds

The consequence of the growing importance of hope to both critical and policy discourses is that the world of appearances becomes increasingly fetishised. This fetishisation can be seen in all discourses of resilience, and of sensitivity and responsivity to feedback effects. No matter whether these discourses are expressed via radical plural and decolonial approaches or by leading policy institutions, the assumption that feedback effects are immediately apparent and available is fetishistic. There can be no direct, one-to-one relation of cause-and-effect that literally works in such unmediated ways. This would be like imagining that if the rainfall was usually heavy one day it was a personal message to you that you should recycle more to help mitigate global warming. The idea that individuals and communities are responsible for their economic, societal and environmental circumstances is racialising; it is a form of, in Adorno's words, 'ontologising the ontic', reinterpreting social and historical outcomes of economic and social inequality or of climate change as products of the inner attributes of peoples and societies.

Once communities or societies are understood to be held back by their lack of resilience, as an inner capacity for agential becoming, for their resignation to what exists, for their lack of 'hope' or inability to hope well, they are then required to be capacity-built. Hope and resilience are interconnected in that, without the underpinning of hope, resilience would lack conceptual coherence in its ontological framing, centring the relational and 'internal' properties of the subject. While resilience may be increasingly ubiquitous across the policy spectrum, it is actually the enrolment of hope that does the work of rationalisation and explanation (see, for example, Hutcheson 2025). Inner capacities cannot be seen directly; they can only be seen indirectly and retrospectively. It is only after the event, after the trauma or the catastrophe (or after its avoidance or mitigation) that it can be said that the individual or community possessed the capacity to hold the future open, to construct relations that were able to have a futural purchase or impact. Hope provides the ontological assumptions that enable the capacities- and capabilities-based discourses of resilience, which are not about knowing, controlling and directing but training responsivities in relation to contingent or unexpected events.

The key point being made by Adorno, in the problematisation of critical discourses of aesthesis as world-making, is that the attempt to celebrate particular modes of survivance – different community practices or traditions or creative and innovative modes of experimentation – is inevitably going to be counter-productive. Firstly, there is a construction of a mode of being in the world which is assumed to be 'authentic', 'resilient', 'worlding otherwise'; in which case the assumption is that the capacities and capabilities that enabled this can be learnt or developed elsewhere, providing a mode of critical problem-solving. Secondly, there is the implicit assumption that if there is a solution to the problems of the contemporary world, then this is not one that comes from the development of technical and scientific expertise or from the provision of national and international resources but rather is one based on the work of hoping well as an open-ended mode of responsivity. When hope is drawn upon in ways that associate inner powers and capacities with the appearances of the world as such, or with certain traditions and practices, or with specific communities and societies, then it is a small step to the fetishisation of *this* world of appearances and the essentialisation or responsibilisation of marginalised communities and individuals.

RACE AND ONTOLOGICAL AMBIGUITY

The first two modes of enrolling hope in alternative, critical and emancipatory projects – considered in the first half of this book, were oriented around reenchanting the human as subject, either via libidinal drives or freeing the imagination. Both suffered from abstraction and idealism. The desire to keep open alternative futures against the closures of repressive social and political constraints – despite disillusionment with, or exclusion from, formal modes of political participation – resulted in highly idealised subject-centred understandings of agency where the material world was secondary. Yet, as seen above, attempts to bring in the materiality of the world and to ground human agency within specific communities of experience brings with it the problems of essentialism and responsibilisation, ontologising the ontic, as the appearance of the world enables judgements about human capacities and capabilities. This section therefore considers some work that seeks to open up the problematic of hope's 'ontological ambiguity'.[3]

Perhaps a starting point for engaging with the problem of hope and ontological ambiguity could be Claire Colebrook's analysis, 'Toxic Feminism: Hope and Hopelessness after Feminism' (2010). Colebrook is sensitive to the problem of identifying the politics of hope with specific communities or identities, in fine:

> The concept of woman is therefore tied to the structure of hope insofar as it is at once essential for any radical politics to have some claim, from the present, for the

> future; and yet woman also prevents that future from being absolutely open.
>
> (Colebrook 2010, 323)

In articulating a privileged identity position, the present is problematised, but the future is limited in its openness, to more of the same. Once second-wave and difference feminisms sought to go beyond the recognition or the inclusion of women and realised the need to challenge patriarchy as a structuring condition of the world, the problem became precisely that of distinguishing 'between woman as she existed in actuality and woman in potentiality' (2010, 324). In which case, the subject at the centre of the politics of hope becomes part of the problem, making hope's ontological grounding a barrier to imaginaries of other possible worlds.

According to Colebrook, the politics of hope became bifurcated between those feminists who had plenty of hope, for recognition and inclusion, and those who sought to challenge essentialising constructions of gender who are seen to have abandoned hope and have turned to utopian imaginaries of futures which are no longer connected to struggles in the present, so:

> For Butler, there can be no "woman" without the heterosexual matrix that brings with it familial and Oedipal norms. Feminism becomes a war on images and normativity, and in doing so, implicitly annihilates its *raison d'être*, its hope. It aims to have no place or being other than its pure mobility. It effaces (what I will defend later as) a radical Platonism or radical essentialism, where essences refer to potentialities that are not reducible to the subject, which is nothing more than the ongoing act of its own purely formal becoming.
>
> (Colebrook 2010, 327)

Colebrook argues that feminist hope is torn between a conservative or reformist 'optimism' that projects the present into the future positively and a 'utopianism' that effaces the importance of gender in imaginaries of becoming without limits. The problem of hope lies precisely in its conjunction with the political, with its need to be grounded in a political subject, here in the category of 'woman':

> "Woman" acts as the hinge of hope: it is because there is something like woman, not fully subsumed by patriarchy, that one might hope for things to be otherwise; but it is also because hope is the hope *of* this figure of woman that the future is always somehow not fully open or radically utopian, but in part bounded by the present. This inescapably figural contamination of feminist hope causes feminism to appear as hopeless: without some figure of woman, there would be nothing to hope for — no sense that woman requires some different future from the present — but it is that same figure that precludes hope from imagining a future beyond any of its current figures.
>
> (Colebrook 2010, 331)

The problem with articulations of hope within ethico-political projects of becoming otherwise is that there has been little attempt to analyse the stakes of ontological ambiguity. This means that hope, as an attempt to hold open alternative futures, has a powerful critique of the world but it is not clear whether it is possible to escape from the two problems, highlighted in the Introduction and here by Colebrook, of either falling into the trap of optimism (reifying the world that exists) or utopianism (disavowing or denying this world). Both optimism and utopianism end up subordinating any alternative future to *this* world, rather than challenging it:

> Feminism, if it has any sense, is structured by a hope grounded on some figure from the present; in order to hope for something like a new woman, a new mode of femininity, or a transformation of women as they

> are (under patriarchy) to women as they might be, one necessarily draws upon the present. It maps out some future that is at once other than the present and yet referenced to an unfulfilled actuality of the present. At the same time, there also has to be a negation or hopelessness directed towards the present, a sense of the inadequacy of any current figure or norm.
>
> (Colebrook, 2010, 332)

Colebrook argues that hope's liminal position, of critique of what exists at the same time as enabling the construction of worlds to come, needs to be wary of the double trap of either 'optimistic' apologia, affirming subjects and identities, romanticising or essentialising marginalised groups and communities, or 'utopian' disavowal, dismissing identities as false constructions, taking the liberal universalist position of being colour- or gender-blind. In essence, then, the problem with alternative ethicopolitical practices underpinned by hope is that of the relation between hope and *this* broken world, in which hope appears to be all that is left. Framings that draw upon hope thereby risk reproducing not only the world and the subject of modernity but also modernity's racialising ordering of the 'global colour line' (Du Bois 2018; Silva 2007), despite attempts to do politics 'otherwise'.

This problem with hope is not always as clear as in Colebrook's analysis. One reason for this is that 'optimism', or apologia, the racialising 'ontologising of the ontic', which assumes that communities form distinct 'worlds' or a 'pluriverse', does not always appear as 'optimism' and often does not appear as racialising, particularly when expressed by decolonial scholars and critical theorists of the pluriverse (on this problematic, see Davidson 2024). One example of the successful problematisation of pluriversal assumptions of autonomous worlds has been the work of Metis scholar Matt Gravlin, who has sought to challenge discourses which draw upon hope to underpin Indigenous imaginaries of world-making through 'grounded normativity' (2024).

Gravlin suggests that Simpson's articulation of hope underpinning the ethicopolitical project of Indigenous 'grounded normativity' constructs acts of refusal and resistance of Indigenous peoples in problematic ways (for a discussion of Simpson's understanding see Chapter 2). This is because many Indigenous communities fail to become Indigenous in these ways, fail to thrive and to become strong and healthy Indigenous nations. He asks whether this means that these communities lack inner strength and Indigenous capacities, that, somehow, they might fail to be 'truly Indigenous' (2024, 10). Gravlin writes: 'The opening of an Indigenous ontological plane in the manner described by Simpson can be seen to perform a[n]… internalization of the world and confine indigeneity to another brand of essentialism, simultaneously' (2024, 12). Perhaps, most importantly, Gravlin highlights the limits of the self-realising ethicopolitical imaginary of world-making:

> Simpson delimits resistance and binds it to an essential difference of indigeneity that, when embodied by peoples, requires no interaction with or response to colonial powers. This calls into being a subject who is either immune to, and outlives the material conditions of settler colonialism, or one who succumbs and expires in its allegiance to it… In the alternative world proposed by Simpson there is no need to overcome obstacles such as dispossession and poverty. To access this world is to reside where all that is needed is immediately available through Indigenous intelligence systems and where ideals of material or temporal progress are abandoned.
>
> (Gravlin 2024, 13–14)

Gravlin draws attention to the limits of worlding as a futural project: 'Where the materiality of the outer world is subordinated to our psychic abilities to suffer its presence. And reality becomes a phenomenological construction' (2024, 14). This limit is precisely that of the denial and disavowal of the materiality of the world that structures and overdetermines the actions of the 'world-making' subject. As Gravlin states: 'Grounded normativity, as it is presented in this way, does not liberate Indigenous peoples from colonial power, but conditions their survival in a world to which there is no alternative' (2024, 15). The consequence of utilising hope in this way, as expressed in processual projects of holding open alternative futures, is the underlining that there is no alternative to worlding the world that exists. The irony is that discourses of 'decolonising' and 'liberating' minds become merely an invitation for new and further forms of intervention aimed at 'developing' or 'capacity-building' the non-resilient subject, the subject incapable of becoming truly Indigenous or of enabling a Queer futurity of infinite becoming.

As Rei Terada highlights (2023), today communities are seen to be problematic and in need of guidance and intervention if they are not sufficiently open to the world of hope, resilience and adaptation. As Matt Gravlin makes clear in his discussion of Indigenous resurgence, and Frantz Fanon earlier articulated in *Black Skin, White Masks* (1986 [1952]), for those racialised as other, modes of relational practice which are underpinned by hope, present a double bind. Hope is articulated via distinct modes of relational and affective being- and becoming-with in a world of radical opening, yet the human as an abstraction still remains at the centre of this imaginary. Thus, as Bobby Benedicto argues, the capacity to hope well necessarily appears as an unmarked 'white privilege' while the cut between hoping well and hoping badly is projected onto those who lack these attributes. Thus:

> Here a familiar schema emerges, in which the erotics of death appears as a dangerous luxury, as the proclivity of those who would find relative security in the gap

> between psychic dissolution and physical death, between the figurative and the literal: a matter, that is, of (white) privilege. In turn, the queer of color emerges as a generative figure, a bearer of hope; lauded for its resilience amid the perils that surround it, its interests appear to lie not in the dream of a deadly unbinding but in staving off the threat of death by undertaking the revivifying labor of creation—of world making—or what might be understood, more critically, as the burden of repairing the very world that demands its annihilation.
>
> (Benedicto 2019, 277–278)

In *Black Skin, White Masks*, Chapter 5, 'The Fact of Blackness', Fanon makes the point that projecting upon those racialised as Black, differential capacities and capabilities but changing the signs of those distinctions from negative (less-than-human) to positive (more-than-human) of being able to access psychic or imaginative capacities or to have 'poetic' capabilities of openness, of access and relation, is just as racialising:

> The soul of the white man was corrupted, and, as I was told by a friend who was a teacher in the United States, "The presence of the Negroes beside the whites is in a way an insurance policy on humanness. When the whites feel that they have become too mechanized, they turn to the men of colour and ask them for a little human sustenance." At last I had been recognized, I was no longer a zero.
>
> (Fanon 1986, 129)

The struggle over the right way of being human, the right way of being in relation to the world, over 'worlding' as a mode of overcoming modernist closures, hierarchies and blind spots, is one in which those ontologically excluded from (human) being can never be on an equal playing field. These divisions are merely reproduced in a different register of expectation, one in which, as Gravlin states, Indigenous communities are expected to be 'truly

Indigenous' in their resilience and self-reliance or be seen to have failed themselves. As Fanon states:

> So here we have the Negro rehabilitated... "standing before the bar," ruling the world with his intuition, the Negro recognized, set on his feet again, sought after, taken up, and he is a Negro—no, he is not a Negro but the Negro, exciting the fecund antennae of the world, placed in the foreground of the world, raining his poetic power on the world... Somewhere beyond the objective world of farms and banana trees and rubber trees, I had subtly brought the real world into being. The essence of the world was my fortune. Between the world and me a relation of coexistence was established.
>
> (Fanon 1986, 127–128)

The process of worlding 'otherwise' takes a critical, aesthetic or speculative form of seeking to undo, unmake or divest the human as subject, but is still highly subject-centred, enabling a more 'authentic' human subject to become in *this* world. However, this is a radicalism that focuses on the subject rather than the world. One which draws on a romanticised understanding of authentic Man, seeking to return to the innate, authentic capacities of the unalienated subject, in tune with their relational environment but also drawing upon a radical critique of the present. Theodor Adorno argued that:

> The talk about man makes itself popular in the old-fashioned, half-timbered, gable-roof way. But it also wins friends in a more contemporary way, in the gesture of a radicalism which wants to dismantle whatever merely conceals, and which concerns itself with the naked essence that hides under all cultural disguises. However, as it is a question of Man and not, for the sake of men, of the conditions which are made by men and which harden into opposition against them, we are released from criticizing them.
>
> (Adorno 2003, 48–49)

The ethicopolitical claims for an open futurity focus on liberating Man through enabling inner, immanent capacities that have been repressed by the modernist order. For Adorno, this is an essentialising move, which reifies the understanding of the human rather than historicising it in relation to its societal conditions (2003, 50). What is essentialised is not some particular trait or capacity but the capacity for self-making, for self-determination, held to distinguish the human from the nonhuman, lacking in self-making agency. The subject would always and already have the capacity for freedom, and all that would be necessary would be to 'choose freedom' rather than repression. This is precisely the racialising cut of the human from the non-human, the self-determined from the other-determined (Silva 2007).

From this perspective, ethicopolitical projects informed by hope contain at their core racial apologia; in fine, they emphasise the agential and choice-making capacity of the subject in abstraction from the racialised historical and social conditions of this subject's construction. In this bifurcatory way, Kantian binary imaginaries of the self- and other-determined subject ground the 'authentic', idealised, human as an adaptive subject, open-endedly coping with life's challenges. As Tryone Palmer argues, this imaginary of 'worlding' has clear racialising overtones whereby 'World(ing) is an achievement, a capacity, that Blackness is rendered as fundamentally lacking by definition' (2020, 259). The process of enabling and capacity-building assumes, as both pre-condition and as retroactive justification, the idea that inner resources, underpinned by 'hope', are required for subjects to cope with, struggle against, and to succeed in the midst of challenges and contingencies.

For Adorno, the capacity to choose to world the world otherwise, central to hope's imbrication within aesthetic praxes of world-making (see Andriote 2024), is at the core of the problem with the agency-centred focus of holding open alternative futures. The subject is portrayed as politically and aesthetically worlding itself through drawing out its inner capacities for attunement and relational sensibility, but this is necessarily a process where the unconscious or inner self is ontologically assumed to be instrumentally available at the ontic level of conscious awareness or affective affinity, attuned to other non-human modes of existence.[4] Attention to determinate modes of being is seen as crucial yet always underneath them another, more authentic mode of being in and open to relation, is presupposed.

The contradiction or gap between facticity, the world of appearance, and the subject is attributed to blockages at the level of subjectivity itself (Adorno 2003, 96). Adorno describes this, as stated earlier, as ontologising the ontic, making the present all that there is:

> By the fact that it is ontological, the alternative of authenticity and inauthenticity directs itself according to whether someone decides for himself or not. It takes its directive, beyond real states of affairs, from the highly formal sense of belonging to oneself. Yet, its consequences in reality are extremely grave. Once such an ontology of what is most ontic has been achieved, philosophy no longer has to bother about the societal and natural-historical origin of this title deed, which declares the individual owns himself.
>
> (Adorno 2003, 94)

The agent-centred approach, which in seeking to go beyond facticity, grounds itself on the inner capacity of the subject or community to reason or relate otherwise, falls back into tautology, whereby self-identity becomes an:

> ...unlosable element, which has no substratum but its own concept, the tautological selfness of the self, is to provide the ground, as Heidegger puts it, which the authentics possess and the inauthentics lack. The essence of Dasein, i.e., what is more than its mere existence, is nothing but its selfness: it is itself.
>
> (Adorno 2003, 95)

The problematic and oppressive reality remains, and rather than empirical reality being transcended 'it transforms a bad empirical reality into transcendence' (Adorno 2003, 95). Adorno considers the radical ethicopolitical calls, underpinned by hope – to 'become what you are', 'to be open to encounter' etc. – to be a soulless 'jargon of authenticity', no different to the world of advertising slogans and 'mindfulness clinics', selling individualist solutions that idealistically assume that the subject literally worlds its world outside of any determining reality: 'Subjectivity, Dasein itself, is sought in the absolute disposal of the individual over himself, without regard to the fact that he is caught up in a determining objectivity' (Adorno 2003, 105). Once the individual is understood to be in the process of self-emancipation, enabling their inner and authentic self to emerge through open-ended encounters with alterity, there can be no separation between this process of 'worlding' and the condition of 'freedom' as another mode of subordination (see also Yountae 2017, 105).

CONCLUSION

It would seem that what remains of the project of reenchanting the subject is merely its exhausted afterlife. In the words of Donna Haraway, ethicopolitical projects, underpinned by hope, increasingly seek to 'stay with the trouble' of modernity, aware that it is not possible to disavow modernity or to avoid complicity with and implication within it. As Vanessa Manchado de Oliviera argues in *Hospicing Modernity* (2021), this is more a matter of letting go, neither of saving the world of modernity nor of seeking to bring it down, but of practicing love and care in the present. Openness to the world and the development of 'response-abilities' are not so much about instrumental changes as adapting to what is, 'disinvesting' and working on the 'decolonization of our unconscious desires' (2021, 239). You could not get much further from hope's earlier imbrication within agendas of liberating unconscious desires from modernity's 'surplus-repression' (Marcuse 1987, 35). The resilient subject is required to draw upon hope and to continually emancipate itself from its limits and barriers, but this is a struggle that is suborned to the present merely reimagined as an open futurity.

This desire to undo, to unmake, to welcome entropy rather than to struggle against it, can be seen in a range of works, from Roy Scranton's *Learning to Die in the Anthropocene* (2015) to Dougald Hine's *At Work in the Ruins* (2023) and Alexis Shotwell's *Against Purity* (2016). It may be the end of *the* world but it's not the end of everything, these critical thinkers argue. There is still a subject and there is still a temporality, a 'to come'. In this context, hope is not drawn upon in order to save the world or to build a new world in its ruins, but for the recognition that entanglement means there is no escape from the closures of the Anthropocene as the contemporary condition. Perhaps a theorist who most exemplifies this perspective is Alexis Pauline Gumbs, particularly in her well-cited book *Undrowned: Black Feminist Lessons from Marine Animals* (2020). Here, there is no mourning for the loss of modernist imaginaries that cut societies from their relationships and embedded ecologies. The task of holding open alternative futures is not merely a matter of struggle and resistance but also of shared care and love; a matter of learning to 'listen across species, across extinction, across harm' (2020, 15).

Gumbs' book is one which draws upon hope for ethical or poetic practices of unmaking or undoing the human, enabling work on the self that opens up ways of living and identifying with others. This is a book for 'everyone who knows that a world where queer Black feminine folks are living their most abundant, expressed, and loving lives is a world where everybody is free' (Gumbs 2020, 13). Freedom is not a matter of fighting the world, of mastering it, but of surrendering to it. 'Freedom' thereby depends upon the support of hope, on the openness of the now:

> AND WHAT HAPPENS IF WE just let go? Like dolphins who beach themselves on shore to eat, and trust the tide to bring them back into the water, or who time their birth cycles to seasonal floods, or migrate across the world following warm currents on a menopausal planet. What it would take to tune in with our environment enough to be in flow with the Earth, instead of in struggle against it.
>
> (Gumbs 2020, 121)

Ethicopolitical projects, informed by hope, have facilitated alternatives to a liberal political imaginary, and have been powerfully expressed in the Black radical tradition, in Queer studies, in subaltern studies and in other political imaginaries, dependent upon a drive of becoming in the world. A mode and form of being such that the world needed to be otherwise for the promise of this becoming to be realised; for new genres of the human to emerge, for the telos of marginalised identities to be enabled. Thus, at stake in the enrolment of hope in the underpinning of these projects, was not really their content per se, but rather the temporal ontology of becoming in which the subject's sense of self in relation to the world was central. Hope thereby informed radical praxes where affirmation of the subject took a negative form of the rejection of identity and of fixity. However, now perhaps it can be argued that hope was only radical in relation to these projects' sense of subjectivity, or 'entitlement' if you will. Hope, understood as underscoring the motivation, the drive, the desire, to draw upon the potentiality that exists beyond the immediate 'manifestation of the world that *is*' was dependent on the legacies of the modern subject. As the legacy of the modern subject has grown ever fainter, this has increasingly denuded left projects of hope of their positive transformative content.

NOTES

1 Please note that the page numbers for Grove (2018) refer to a pre-publication manuscript.
2 There is the difficulty that the discourse of aesthetic enablement sets up a problematic divide between those able to design themselves 'authentically' and those still held back by the closures of regimes of representation. While design is held to enable those who are still constrained, how the designers manage to free themselves is still left in question. This is not really adequately addressed by assumptions that designers need to be able to carry out their own 'inner work' in order to meet these challenges (see, for example, Escobar 2017, 157, 246, n.15; see also Chandler 2024b).
3 As will become clear, 'ontological ambiguity' is used as a placeholder to highlight the problem of utilising hope while seeking to avoid the slip to the ontic (thereby replacing hope with optimism) or, alternatively abstracting from structural constraints (and thereby replacing hope with utopianism).
4 Thus, Jasbir Puar writes that: 'Affect is precisely the body's hopeful opening, a speculative opening not wedded to the dialectic of hope and hopelessness but rather a porous affirmation of what could or might be' (2017, 19).

4

HOPE AGAINST HOPE

INTRODUCTION

In the previous chapter, the ontological ambiguity at the centre of ethicopolitical projects informed by hope was highlighted as a key question. This ambiguity came increasingly to the fore as these projects appeared to lose their transformatory aspirations, understanding open futures as already baked into processual understandings of the present. Modes of critical praxis, underpinned by hope, seeking to oppose the multiple closures of our broken worlds, appear to have increasingly exhausted their radical potential. As analysed above, the enrolling of hope in contemporary projects is increasingly governmentalised, in programmes of international and domestic political regulation, as much as in critical imaginaries. The problem of alternative ethicopolitical projects is that both the world and the human subject are affirmed as excessive, as full of potentialities, as plenitudes. This was highlighted through the examination of three modes of alternative ethicopolitical praxis, underpinned by hope – focused upon the libidinal drives, freedom dreams and relational responsivities – all of which posited the return to lost capacities, harmonies and dispositions. While these approaches provided a critique of the world as it appears they also tended to affirm a past set of potentialities for emancipation, immanent to the human or to relationality.

DOI: 10.4324/9781003632719-7

This chapter analyses the problem at the heart of enrolling hope into alternative ethicopolitical praxes. In fine, the desire to transcend the present increasingly appears as a preserving or correcting move, rather than one of radical refusal or resistance. Thus, hope could be understood as working in these framings to transform drives of negation into those of affirmation. The problem of affirming *this* world and the subject as constituted in modernity is revisited, using the example of the argument of Rebecca Solnit and the critique of Joseph Winters' 'black melancholia'. The following section analyses how the utilisation of hope has been problematised in attempts that seek to disarticulate the subject to avoid the ontological trap of essentialising and responsibilising marginalised groups. The second half of the chapter illustrates 'hope against hope' via a brief consideration of 'Queer negativity', 'Crip negativity' and 'Black nihilism', three approaches that seek to highlight and refuse the disastrousness of the world rather than move to disavow it.

AFFIRMATION

Jean-François Lyotard, in *Libidinal Economy* (2004 [1974]), argues that restricting a critical, libidinal, focus to the mind of the individual subject in the absence of a broader engagement with the social and material relations of society is problematic. Even if Freud is radicalised so that libidinal desire is affirmed as a transformative power, rather than merely a product of a lack, the force of potentiality is constrained and captured by the subject and thus reproduces the modernist game of power and control (Samman 2023, 12). The potential for moving beyond or operating outside a modernist political imaginary is lost. In this respect, for Lyotard, Marx provides a better model for critique, as the proletariat are not structurally a force of immanent affirmation but only of negation. The proletariat, for Marx, are not a radical force because of some inherent or lost capacity that can be affirmed or recognised. There is no wrong done to them that could be righted by inclusion, recognition or status rewards. The proletariat are purely a negative or negating force.

For the theorists of projects of keeping open alternative futures, underpinned by hope, marginal subjects are necessarily 'positively present in modern society, not negatively' (Lyotard 2004, 121). 'The marginals are libidinal affirmations, the proletarians were negations of negation in a journey and a sublation' (Lyotard 2004). Lyotard argues that 'this small detail', this '"methodological" nuance' creates an ontological problem of separation (2004, 121), as if there could be a social force somehow external to the world as it exists, or some 'external reference', some set of separations between a pure or non-modern agency and the agencies enrolled in the reproduction of the world as it appears. For Lyotard, the problem of enrolling hope into these projects of alternative critique is that they necessarily seek to suture, to close, the gap between alienated experience of the world and the world as such. This gap is always interpreted as problematic, as a falsehood, obscuring the true reality of harmonious becoming. Instead, he argued, the gap should be opened further; the true reality is the problem of the world not something lacking in the subject. If the subject is capable of resisting this world, and its appearances, then perhaps it can resist the call to adapt and become otherwise, to suborn itself to what is.

Kafka famously pointed out to (his friend and publisher) Brod that there was 'plenty of hope, an infinite amount of hope – but not for us' (Benjamin 2015a, 112–113). What Kafka implied was that despite living in this world, the capacity to become otherwise, was denied to them as Jewish intellectuals in 1920s Prague, alienated from both German culture and their Jewish heritage. To become as a Jew and a German was not possible in *this* world; this mode of being could no longer exist. Hope was for others, not for them. The only 'becoming other' on offer was that of physical and ontological annihilation. Struggles to hold open alternative futures, informed by hope, may be possible in the world, but capacities to imagine this are not evenly distributed. Furthermore, the capacity to hope to 'become other', to move beyond or apposite to any fixed identity, to escape the 'carceral categories' of modernity, is not open to all.

In today's struggles against the multiple closures of broken worlds, discourses of hope articulate the subject as always becoming other, as never fixed or finalised. All that remains after this deconstruction is the libidinal desire for alterity, for worlding otherwise, for otherwise worlds. What is conflated here is particular concrete subjects and abstract imagined ones. While the imagined subject can be envisioned as 'worlding' its world, capable of pursuing its desires and interests without internal blockage, much like a stoloniferous plant sends out tendrils for sustenance (Roy 2018), real, living, subjects tend to have no such modes of unalienated articulation.[1] Imaginaries of 'worlding' understand the subject within relational processes of becoming that efface the necessity of an ontological cut between the alienated present and an unalienated future. A stoloniferous plant has no relation to liberal constructions of the world of rights and freedoms, whether there is democracy or dictatorship makes no difference to its affective and hopeful openness to 'becoming itself'.

Perhaps, for the liberal academic, representing the virtual subject in a virtual world, becoming can be experienced as affirmation, in this way. Discovering the wonderous nature of the everyday, being a caring member of the community, refusing to eat meat or to buy the latest media subscription – being in the world – then becomes no different to open-ended becoming or to 'freedom dreaming'. This unalienated appreciation of the world can be seen, for example, in Rebecca Solnit's *Hope in the Dark* (2016). Solnit, as discussed above, seeks to see the positives that are always possible to be gleamed from disasters: the brave and selfless acts of resilience after terror attacks or natural disasters; the unintended consequences of Viagra saving the lives of exotic wildlife; successful rewilding after extinctions; the resurgence of protest movements or Indigenous communities. From on high, from her 'God's eye perspective' of the universal, the world of structures and reproduced hierarchies and exclusions fades into the background, and the present becomes 'presenced'.

Solnit argues that for marginalised groups, forced to struggle out of necessity, hope is not a problem; instead, she is writing for 'my people, middle-class white people', those who had become disillusioned or had given up (2016, 139). It seems to her, that for these people 'something more small-scale and sarcastic was the reduced version of the self that remained to us' (Solnit 2016). Ethicopolitical engagements drawing upon hope, having the imagination to see the future in the present, enable Solnit, as she states, 'to see the world in full colour', to accept that this life will never be perfect but that the future is not yet written (2016, 140). Unlike Kafka, Solnit's world is full, and she is a self-fulfilled subject within it, able to appropriate for herself the past, the present and the future. Solnit goes regularly to the New York UN Plaza, to buy food from farmers and again to give it away to the destitute, where she visits 'with a young monk from San Francisco Zen Centre to feed the people' who gather (2016, 113):

> This is what the world looks like to me, like UN Plaza, full of half-forgotten victories and new catastrophes, of farmers and junkies, of mountains of apples and of people trying to change the world and tell the truth. Someday all this may be ruins over which the pelicans will fly, but for now it is a place where history is unfolding. Today is also the day for creation.
>
> (Solnit 2016, 114)

As Kafka states, hope is only enabling for those who are at home in the world as it exists. For those excluded from this world, the libidinal, imaginative or relational investment in *this* world is problematic. This problem of affirmation is addressed directly in Joseph Winters' important contribution to work on hope in critical Black studies, *Hope Draped in Black* (2016). Winters is all too aware of how hope is enrolled to enable a processual ontology of human becoming that is readily enlisted into 'post-racial' imaginaries of alternative futures (2016, 4), downplaying traumatic past and present experiences. He suggests that Black hope or 'melancholic hope' lies precisely in heightening capacities for paying attention 'to remember, register, and contemplate the damages, losses and erasures of the past and present' (2016, 7).

Melancholic approaches to hope thereby seek to hold the future open through unsettling the present sense of the status quo rather than focusing upon consoling futural imaginaries. In articulating this perspective, Winters draws upon Black musical practices, such as spirituals, blues, jazz and hip hop. Key to the argument is that the 'melancholic attachment to the losses and remains of history makes possible a different kind of future than the one imagined by the proponents of progress' (2016, 19). This is because cultivating different modes of attunement and sensitivity 'may also make selves more open to neglected possibilities and novel ways of being within the current order of things' (2016, 83).

The post-racial imagination, very much present in US President Barack Obama's *The Audacity of Hope* (2008), cannot fail to acknowledge mourning, loss and the sense of the tragic, but nevertheless diminishes attunement to this loss and suffering through relying on the liberal state-based political logic of futural progress and inclusion (2016, 190). Obama plays on Du Bois' conception of 'double-consciousness' (2018) in his sensitivity to the gap between the self-imaginary of American exceptionalism and its underside of racial exclusion and disavowal. However, the point that Winters presses on is that this attempt to enfold recognition of past and present trauma into an alternative political project of becoming otherwise cannot avoid disavowing and reproducing the violence constitutive of the American sense of self and of national destiny. *Hope Draped in Black* (2016) therefore presents a very different and more problematising framing than that articulated by Sylvia Wynter in *Black Metamorphosis* (n.d.) considered in Chapter 1.

For Winters, the desire for coherence and harmony, even if constructed as part of the project of open-ended becoming, of being human otherwise, is a problematic way of drawing upon hope. 'These triumphant images prevent the underside of these images from unravelling and undoing our attachments to them, thereby foreclosing a different and more melancholic kind of hope' (2016, 196). Winters suggests that hope should instead be utilised to truly hold the future open rather than assume a telos towards becoming 'infinitely human'. Thus:

> Confronting loss… figuratively wounds us; it exposes and potentially reduces our investment in being coherent selves, communities, and identities… Becoming more open and vulnerable to the agony and torment of others requires us to loosen, rather than tighten, our attachment to reassuring narratives about the genius, uniqueness, and supremacy of our way of life, celebratory narratives that shield us from the unsettling work that mourning can accomplish.
>
> (Winters 2016, 203)

Winters argues that those, like Obama, who seek to enrol the tragic reality of the world into discourses of futurity, or suggest, like Rorty (see this book's Introduction), that we need to have more faith in the political sphere, are mistaken (2016, 211). Also, contra Rorty, he argues that hope can be enrolled in projects of critical deconstruction which can have a constructive component, even if this is indeterminate:

> Leaving the constructive moment indeterminate does not necessarily mean... an unwillingness to imagine a different kind of world; the indeterminate moment with regard to reconstructing the world is an ethical and political strategy that acknowledges and registers the violence involved in well-intentioned endeavors...
>
> (Winters 2016, 244)

Melancholic hope thereby is not about passivity and acceptance but instead 'draws attention to the underside of overconfident notions of self, agency and action', the desire to control, to regulate and to limit the 'Other' (Winters 2016, 244). For Winters, 'a more generous promising world' requires an opening towards wounding and social fractures rather than attempts to escape them; hope thereby can inform understandings of shared vulnerability rather than imaginaries of futural security in becoming otherwise.

This emphasis on the world as it is, rather than how one might wish it to be, returns engagement with hope to the initial concerns of critical theory. For the theorists of the Frankfurt School, Freud had already made this distinction, revealing that the structure of repression was much deeper than the formal and contingent regimes of the political. However, whereas Freud argued that individuals needed to accept and adjust to a world that was necessarily repressive, Frankfurt School thinkers sought to historicise it, linking repression to the modern governmental regime itself, and seeking to go beyond it. For Marcuse, for example, there could be no imaginaries of libidinal, imaginative or relational investment in the self, in community or in the world if it is in *this* world. This would be merely 'idealistic ethics', conforming to the repressive order. To speak of the productive realization of the personality, of care, responsibility, and respect for one's fellow men, of productive love and happiness – as if men could actually practice all this and remain sane and full of "well being" in a society... of *total alienation.* could only be repressive (Marcuse 1987, 258 italics added). He concludes:

> As a result, productiveness, love, responsibility become "values" only in so far as they contain manageable resignation and are practiced within the framework of socially useful activities (in other words, after repressive sublimation); and then they involve the effective denial of free productiveness and responsibility – the renunciation of happiness.
>
> (Marcuse 1987, 259)

Marcuse's critique of 'neo-Freudian revisionism', with which he ends *Eros and Civilization*, is useful to think through the limits of contemporary modes of using hope to underpin struggles to keep open alternative futures in the face of the multiple closures of broken worlds. The problem is not so much a conceptual one but one, as raised at the end of the last chapter, of 'ontological ambiguity'. The ambiguity of processual and relational understandings of open-ended becoming, which depend upon hope, is an ontological one: 'love', 'redress', 'freedom', 'abolition', 'justice', 'community', 'emancipation' etc. can be proclaimed as goals without clarifying whether the aspiration is to achieve these within *this* world or only after the ending of attachments to what exists or is given in appearance.

In Marcuse's understanding, the 'revisionist' neo-Freudians intentionally manipulated hope to play on this ambiguity: 'This ambiguity makes the revisionist philosophy appear to be critical where it is conformist, political where it is moralistic' (1987, 159–160). 'The brute fact of societal repression has transformed itself into a "moral problem"' (1987, 266). While Freud problematically naturalised the repressive condition, he at least recognised the structural nature of repression as a matter of the construction of both the world and the subject; his framework, for Marcuse, was 'eminently critical in so far as it is materialistic' (1987, 273). In the idealistic focus upon freeing or 'decolonising' the mind and the power of the imagination, Marcuse argues that Freud's problematic becomes a moral or 'spiritual' one, 'which conceals the gap that separates the present from the future' (1987, 273).

Hope is mobilised in these critical discourses in a way that 'conceals the gap that separates the present from the future', in that a processual ontology refuses the distinction between actions necessary in *this* world and those that cannot happen until after this world's ending. The key trope of hope within these ethicopolitical praxes, the focus upon 'the future in the present', centres this ontological ambiguity. Practicing the values of 'care, responsibility, and respect for one's fellow men, of productive love and happiness' could only be a product of denial and disavowal in *this* world, for Marcuse, much in the same way as his colleague Adorno argued that it would be barbaric to write poetry after Auschwitz (Schmidt 2013).

CRIP NEGATIVITY

How to hope without reinforcing dominant imaginaries and social hierarchies is at the centre of much critical work on hope. An illustrative example of how this debate begins to ground the arguments of 'hope against hope' is the ongoing discussion within critical Crip studies. Examples that will be analysed to this end are Alison Kafer's influential work engaging the problems of hope and subject positionality in *Feminist, Queer, Crip* (2013) and J. Logan Smilges book *Crip Negativity* (2023). Kafer argues that the enrolment of hope, in critical discourses imagining other worlds are possible, is central to a futural politics of disability (2013). Where the ontological ambiguity of hope comes in is in the need both to problematise the present but also to avoid any reification of the categories in which this is understood.

Kafer writes that the dominant viewpoints on disability are either that disability is a 'pitiable misfortune, a tragedy that effectively prevents one from leading a good life' or that disability is not a barrier to leading a good life but a reason to campaign for better access and resources (2013, 2). She argues that these viewpoints are limited by their focus on the present. If disability is merely a problem to be accepted or mitigated, there can be no other world that is possible that contains disability; if it did, it would be 'a future that bears too many traces of the ills of the present to be desirable' (2013, 2). In a framing that shares much with Colebrook's discussion of hope and feminism (discussed in Chapter 3), she argues that there is either an abstract vision of the human where disability no longer exists or there is a romanticising, essentialising vision of disability as enabling.

Without challenging ableist assumptions, futural imaginaries can easily write disabled people out of the future entirely, '(preventing them from ever coming into existence) while ignoring the needs and experiences of disabled people in the present' (Kafer 2013, 29). In these discourses, as Kafer states, 'disability cannot appear as anything other than failure' (Kafer 2013). Kafer powerfully critiques utopian imaginaries where 'a world free of impairment is portrayed as a goal shared by all, a goal that is beyond question or analysis, a goal that is natural rather than political' (2013, 74). The task, as Kafer poses it:

> ...is not so much to refuse the future as to imagine disability and disability futures otherwise, as part of other, alternate temporalities that do not cast disabled people out of time, as the sign of the future of no future.
>
> (Kafer 2013, 34)

She argues that her aim is to articulate the politics of disability as both critical and futural, that not only disability cannot be written out of a politics of hope but that disability is, in fact, central to this project: 'In imagining more accessible futures, I am yearning for an elsewhere—and, perhaps, an "elsewhen"—in which disability is understood otherwise: as political, as valuable, as integral' (2013, 3).

To do this, Kafer insists on starting from the real lived experiences of disabled people (2013, 32–33). She calls attention to the specificities of these experiences, in ways that prevent any easy generalisation or risk of appropriation, and asks whether, under these conditions: 'Can claiming crip be a method of imagining multiple futures, positioning "crip" as a desired and desirable location regardless of one's own embodiment or mental/psychological processes?' (2013, 13). The reason why crip can provide such potential vantage points is precisely because of real differentiated lived experiences. These can potentially offer differing phenomenological insights and affectivities that can point towards an ethicopolitical struggle, underpinned by hope, that not only challenges dominant ableist norms but also politically opens up many aspects of everyday life (Kafer 2013). It is the vulnerabilities, sensitivities and affectivities of those classed as disabled that are alleged to be able to shine a new light on societal relations, modes of work, communication and travel, and modes of enjoying the environment (2013, 38).

Open-ended futurity, incompleteness and disability necessarily, logically, imply each other not because disability always requires 'curing' but because emancipation always requires thinking outside and beyond ableist, or any other kind of, normativity. A key example is imagining a different relation to the environment, where natural obstacles are no longer tests for proving capacities and capabilities but rather sites 'of connection or relation' (2013, 143). In this way, it is possible to 'recognize disability experiences and human limitations as essential, not marginal or tangential, to questions about "nature" and environmental movements' (2013, 148). It therefore follows that attempts to eliminate disability also foreclose alternative futures by assuming that what meets the standards of the norm is natural and that its reproduction is a purely natural act rather than a political one (Kafer 2013, 82).

Crip politics of critique aspire to continually problematise and to keep open hegemonic understandings of 'diversity' which seek to see some differences as fortuitous and to be proliferated but others as problematic and to be erased or excluded. Eliminating disability is a move to closure rather than open-ended possibility, eliminating ways of being and experiences that 'can potentially lead to productive insights about intimacy, relationship, and interdependence' (2013, 83). 'To eliminate disability is to eliminate the possibility of discovering alternative ways of being in the world, to foreclose the possibility of recognizing and valuing our interdependence' (Kafer 2013). Rather than 'praising disabled people for overcoming their disabilities' (2013, 97) critical crip approaches seek to utilise the experience of disability to imagine different ways of being and becoming in the world.

While Kafer criticises dominant approaches to disability for being too trapped in the present, and therefore unable to take the distance required for a critical political engagement that does not reproduce contemporary constraints and concerns, Kafer herself has been criticised by other critical crip theorists for precisely the same limitation. J. Logan Smilges argues that Kafer's desire to enable futural imaginaries of other possible worlds, through focusing on a processual open-endedness, both explicitly and implicitly requires people with disabilities to demonstrate capacities for usefulness, for insight, and for imagining relations otherwise. People classified as disabled are required to do the work of salvage and to hold out potential possibilities for futural transformation despite the fact that this world is shaped and determined by ableist principles and understandings. Smilges argues that: 'It is a politics of futurity that requires, at the very least, a will to believe that a better future is possible, as well as the strength to keep trudging toward it' (2023, 24).

In basing critical crip futural imaginaries on real disabled bodily experiences of being in the world, Kafer can be seen to be problematically too 'present' in the world (too 'optimistic'). At this level of real experiential becoming, the world is all too present for the disabled subject. However, the more that Kafer argues that politics is baked into the structures, both material and immaterial, that shape the relations in which people with disability engage with the world, the less sense it makes to argue for a political and relational approach to disability. As Smilges argues, this ethicopolitical enrolment of hope paradoxically tends, often without intention, firstly, to essentialise and to instrumentalise people with disabilities – as having particular capacities and characteristics, even if these are seen as positively enabling – and secondly, to actually reduce the perceived centrality of disability to hegemonic constructions of the human as subject and the world as its object.

The starting point for this framing of critical crip futurity, argues Smilges, underestimates the extent of the problem, as experience alone is not enough to grasp the work that disability does in the construction of *this* world. Smilges argues that the problem is not phenomenological but ontological:

> Institutions and systems such as public education, the workforce, the field of medicine, and the law were not merely made to serve abled people best; they were built on the explicit disavowal of disability. The humanist project that emerged during the Enlightenment era exalts the nondisabled bodymind as an essential characteristic of white supremacy... Along with cisheterosexuality, ability functions as a central pillar of whiteness and thus lies at the core of what it means to be a proper citizen and a productive consumer in the West. No amount of integration can undo the violence woven into the threads of the world as we know it.
>
> (Smilges 2023, 7)

The logic of Smilges' argument is that the ethicopolitical work of reimagining disability as enabling alternative worlds to come into being – worlds in which social, economic and political relations between people, relations with technological enhancements and questions of the environment are reimagined – contains within its assumptions already implicated within the humanist project. In other words, using hope in this way, to enable disability to do the productive work of open-ended processual politics, enabling other worlds to come into being, risks merely reproducing the same blind-spots and closures as earlier critical feminist projects which sought to imagine away some differences while celebrating others. The reason for this is, for Smilges, precisely the grounding of ethicopolitical critique in the experiences of real people and real communities of practice and struggle. This is because engaging at this level, the politics of disability risks essentialising and naturalising categories and understandings, meaning that the desire to hold open alternative futures through the focus on the human as an open-ended processual subject can, in fact must, end up making other worlds less rather than more possible.

Smilges states, that as much as it is possible to 'share in Kafer's optimism for disability's queer volatility, I am wary of the sleight of hand that attempts to reconcile disability's ontological violence without engaging the specific conditions that gave rise to the reclamation of disability itself' (2023, 12). By this Smilges does not just mean the term 'disability'; pivoting away from 'disability' towards 'crip' is not in itself any solution to the problem of assimilation of 'disability' within neoliberal and liberal agendas, unless it addresses what Smilges calls 'disability's ontological crisis' (2023, 17–18). The problem of ontology is precisely the problem which is centred when critical futural approaches are premised upon real experiences and struggles: the problem of a conflation of a phenomenological or ontic question with an ontological one.

For Smilges, a futural politics of disability, is required to draw upon hope differently, in order to reject 'disability' or 'crip' as terms that are used literally to ascribe identities or capacities to specific people (while denying them to others) (2023, 18).

For Smilges, 'crip' can work with hope if it seeks to do different work to 'disability', this work 'includes directly contesting the category of disability itself, especially its (neo)liberalization' (2023, 18). Rather than starting from phenomenological perspectives alleged to enable other realities to come into vision, *this* world needs to be refused in order for the world to be imagined anew (Smilges 2023). Smilges builds upon the work of Muñoz (engaged in Chapter 1 of this book) and Kafer, highlighting their deployments of negativity in the desire to enable other worlds beyond this one to become possible and emphasises their desire for an open-ended 'crip horizon' (2023, 24). However, Smilges problematises their enrolment of hope, of futurity, as an ever open processual becoming, which disability politics is required to suborn itself to.

The problem with the position of Kafer and others, then, is not the futural political work of problematising the grounding assumptions enabling this world to appear natural or normed but that this project does not go far enough in negating, or rather in excavating, the 'present'. This problem is ontological, stemming from the affirmation of particular capacities or capabilities, held to able to bring other worlds into being while this world so hegemonically shapes futural imaginaries. Smilges argues that starting from the experience of disability itself already presupposes what should be open to question, the world in which '*disability* marks proximity to the normative subject' (2023, 29). Disability is always already a privileged subject position from which it can be imagined that another world is possible but at the same time holds it back. Smilges' point is that *this* world is always already the product of the foundational violence of modernity:

> There is no question that disability and experiences of disablement are often linked to marginalization, but it is also the case that marginalization experienced within the category of *disability* must be read in the context of a humanist project that already excludes some populations from its borders… disability marks proximity to the normative subject, as defined by the latter's presumptive health, cisheteronormativity, class status, and whiteness. Proximity to normativity however near or far, remains measurable within the category of subjectivity, however constricted, that distinguishes the interpellable disabled person from the massified debilitated other.
>
> (Smilges 2023, 28–29)

Disability, in this framing, then is not something that literally exists in the world to set people apart, literally enabling some people to phenomenologically experience a 'second sight', enabling them to bring a different futurity into being, to imagine an otherwise world of relational interdependencies beyond this world of racial capitalist ableism. Disability itself is always already caught up in a world of cuts, rankings, orderings and exclusions. 'By regulating subjectivity, the category of disability operates in concert with white supremacy to adjudicate variations of humanness that shore up the able-normative boundaries of whiteness' (2023, 29).

Smilges helps develop the problematisation of hope's ontological ambiguity, introduced in the previous chapter, shifting the focus on negating the present away from an epistemological question of lived and embodied experience, of phenomenology, of 'sight' or of 'imagination' and towards questions of ontology, 'the function of *disability* as a category of being' (2023, 9 italics in original). Smilges argues that: 'Ableism can dramatically shape the lives of people without access to the category of disability, and ableism routinely operates in conjunction with racism, colonialism, classism, and cisheterosexism in ways that remain illegible under the rubric of *disability*' (2023, 32–33 italics in original; see also the extended discussion of debility in Puar 2017). Ableism is structurally baked into the world ontologically, such that it works at a deeper level than merely that of experiential or phenomenological limitations or the narrow instrumentalism of economic productivity and social subordination (Smilges 2023, 33)

While Smilges centres the importance of ontology and highlights the limits of phenomenological approaches to hope, based upon the experiences and struggles of those marginalised, they do not suggest that hope should be abandoned but rather that hope enrolled in this way, places too high a burden of responsibility on those who are often not best placed to assume it. The problem with alternative modes of ethicopolitical praxis informed by hope is that the processual desire to bring another world into being is one of constant attention, constant care and constant becoming. Hope, utilised in this way, compels work such that those inculcated into being its bearers have no chance to rest, to take a break in their other-oriented politics of relational responsibility. Smilges states: 'Negativity gives me time… not to imagine a future but to breathe myself out of the past' (2023, 25–26).

Smilges seeks to break hope from critique, so that: 'the affective spacetimes generated by bad crip feelings make room for refusal on multiple scales, including the refusal of humanist logics and the refusal of the labor of critique' (2023, 70). They argue that taking time out rather than processual immersion is also important for an ethicopolitical understanding of ways in which hope can be engaged differently. Resting 'lends itself to improving the conditions of our world by giving us the time and space to imagine it differently' (2023, 63–64). Smilges, in this way, seeks to maintain hope through steering a path between optimism and utopianism but only through deferring the problem by taking time out. Another, more radical, negative approach that seeks to escape this ontological bind will be considered in the next section, that of 'hope against hope'.

HOPE AGAINST HOPE

'Hope against hope' is often described as the capacity to hope even when a successful outcome seems unlikely. This form of 'hope against hope' very much fits the 'standard model' of hope, discussed in this book's Introduction. Hope against hope, in relation to alternative ethicopolitical praxes that are underpinned by hope, refers to enabling the capacity for hope while realising that hope is an ontological trap, a 'cruel optimism' (in Laurent Berlant's terms, 2011), reproducing and disavowing the disastrousness of the world rather than addressing it. Alternative ethicopolitical imaginaries which enrol hope do not manage to escape the problems of political ontology, so 'hope against hope' must work to separate hope from the political or set hope to work outside and against the political. Calvin Warren offers 'hope against hope' as political apostasy (2015, 32) while others argue that this break can be read as the 'metapolitics' of the Black Horizon (Chipato and Chandler 2024a).

Ethicopolitical projects informed by hope tend to reinforce the disastrousness of the world rather than challenge it as it becomes increasingly clear that hope cannot be enrolled without being caught up in problems of optimism or utopianism. While discussions of hope in analytical philosophy and social psychology see hope as enabling struggles that find a middle way or a balance between optimism and pessimism that keep subjects engaged and active (as discussed in the introductory chapter), the problematic for political theorists is that of hope's relationship to optimism and utopianism. It is important to emphasise that both optimism and utopianism necessarily ameliorate critique of *this* world in their attempts to coherently move beyond it. Hope is either enrolled in 'utopian' and idealist approaches, oriented around an abstract human subject of infinite 'becoming', whereby the historical, material and structural constraints are ignored, or in 'optimist' approaches of critical phenomenology which responsibilise their subjects as somehow capable of constructing their own 'worlds'. Either the future appears as a blank space capable of infinite possibilities or the present is reimagined to be full of hidden plenitude.

Therefore, as James Bliss writes, rather than seeing hope as successfully underpinning struggles to hold open alternative futures it would be better to 'hope *against* hope… not simply as hope for a different or better world, but as the ardent refusal of this world' (2015, 93). Hope against hope as an alternative ethicopolitical approach seeks to evade hope's ontological ambiguity by refusing to be generative, refusing to reenchant, to remake or unmake the human as subject, or to celebrate human capacities for resilience. In what we could call 'the ontological turn' (Hart, 2020) in critical Queer, Black Feminist, Indigenous, Disability and Crip studies, a range of theorists have sought to develop a different analytic to that of the Black radical tradition and hope's enrolment in imaginaries of processual becoming, seeking to move away from the 'all too human' focus upon becoming, adaptation and survivance.

This shift is perhaps marked by the publication of Saidiya Hartman's *Scenes of Subjection* in 1997,[2] in which she argues against the conflation of politics and the social, against 'antipolitics' in the sphere beyond or outside the formal politics of the state. For Hartman, the problem is the divide of the political and the non-political itself, established based on the racial bifurcation of the human and the less-than-human. In being excluded from the sphere of the political, Hartman argues there was a Black 'counterinvestment in the body as a site of pleasure and the articulation of needs and desire' (1997, 70) but forms of 'redress' within this world could never be a remedy or reparation. The reason for this was that resistance and rule were inseparable from the positionality of the Black subject. There was no normative difference as working to change the world in either mode of practical engagement merely enabled the antiblack world to be simulated as one of shared interests and investments. The lack of recognition of Black needs and interests in the formal political sphere could not be somehow repaired by a libidinal investment in the non-political sphere of 'life' itself.

In placing world alienation at the centre of critical Black studies and problematising liberal constructions of the human as universal subject, Hartman enables a problematisation of hope's enrolment in processual imaginaries of open-ended becoming. For the Black subject, hope is not available as a promise that 'other worlds are possible', merely that survivance in this world continues to reveal the gap between *this* world of 'total alienation' and the promise of unalienated life. Hope against hope concerns discourses which draw upon hope to inform practices which break with critique's imagination of an open and alternative futurity and the world beyond this world as one of infinite plenitude. For the advocates of 'hope against hope', engaged with in this chapter, there are no possibilities of alternative futures that can be salvaged from the closures of broken worlds; there is no world beyond this one. There is therefore no question of 'pre-figurative' or 'process' politics but only of survivance in and against *this* world.

As Lee Edelman writes in *Bad Education* (2022), at the heart of the problematic of the ontological turn is the point made by Calvin Warren (2014, 19) that: 'Whenever we equate an ontological position with an identity formation, we perform the very violence that sustains the antagonism' (cited in Edelman 2022, 31). Edelman implies that the problem with articulations of hope that inform the critical tradition is that they 'positivise' political identities, which are mobile social constructs of stigmatisation (2022, 272, n.128). Working on the ontological level, he clarifies that it is problematic to associate hope with communities of practice that are in the world – and thereby uses quotation marks around phrases such as "Black queer" or "Black" and "queer" when used to indicate specific types of persons – to highlight their catachrestic function as placeholders for ontological exclusion (2022, 270, n.100).

For Edelman, as for others working at the level of ontological critique,[3] this 'ontological exclusion' is a product of the cut between the human and the non-human, between the human and nature, between the human and *the* world. For the world to exist, the human had to be violently constructed as the universal subject able to know and to instrumentalise this world as available object. This symbolic order is thereby cohered or sutured through the mobile distinction between the human, constructed as a rational and self-governing individual, and those constructed as less-than-human, alleged to be unable to develop these capacities and capabilities.

Problematically, from this perspective, hope's enrolment within struggles that seek to hold open alternative futures against the multiple closures of broken worlds, means that these approaches necessarily 'positivise' identities and modes of imagination and community practices of resistance. Often this means, as considered in the previous chapter, literally assigning to them non-modern distinctions of otherness, or capacities and capabilities other to those constructed as belonging to the modern or hegemonic imaginary which necessarily assumes a universal ontology of human and world (see also Chandler and Reid 2019). These approaches seek to problematise the claims of modern ontology and to work otherwise; however, for the theorists of 'hope against hope', this problematisation stops halfway, merely seeking to reimagine the human and the world in more pluralised ways, and thereby constructing new ontological imaginaries of relational entanglement and new hierarchies of exclusion.

The point being made by ontological theorists, across critical Queer, Indigenous, Crip and Black studies, is that the solution is not imagining other, more pluralistic cuts, as if it was possible to choose better or nicer ontologies. The fundamental violence of the making of the human and the world was both an ontological violence and a real socio-historical process, which is then disavowed when it is imagined that problems of social order, race and discrimination are merely 'carceral categories' of our minds that can be dissipated by imagining new genres of human becoming. This 'double bind' is at the centre of Saidiya Hartman's critique; there can be no overcoming the ontological cut of the human from its other in *this* world, no matter how inclusive, how plural, how fluid, the imaginary of hope, nor how open the process of becoming otherwise. For Hartman, antiblackness is ontologically built into liberal constructions of the subject and the division between the public and the private, in ways that 'question whether the rights of man and citizen are realizable or whether the appellation "human" can be borne equally by all"'(1997, 6). As Warren argues, 'any recourse to the Political and its discourse of hope will ultimately reproduce the very metaphysical structures of violence that pulverize black being' (2015, 7).

From this starting position, recent work in critical Black studies has reworked key aspects of the Black radical tradition to seek to evade the problems of effacement and disavowal associated with alternative modes of ethicopolitical praxis underpinned by hope. Firstly, through rejecting what Frank Wilderson calls 'Humanist assumptive logics', which assume that there is such a thing as the universal subject called Human (2020, 41). Afropessimism as a metatheoretical project seeks then to articulate Blackness as a structural positionality existing at a higher level of abstraction operating to reveal how Blackness is used to police and maintain the Human as a social construct (2020, 14).[4] Wilderson follows Frantz Fanon in arguing that the Black lacks ontological standing as a subject and draws on the work of David Marriott (2000) to make clear the implication that this has for articulations of hope:

> Imagine the black man the white man wants you to be... and be him (or, at least, mime him)," David Marriott writes in his treatise on lynching. "[O]ur unconscious... is given over to that work of second-guessing, of dare and double dare. There's no place here for what the black man wants, or for a black unconscious driven by its own desires and aggression.
>
> (Wilderson 2020, 47)

Here, 'Blackness, as a paradigmatic position (rather than as a set of cultural practices or anthropological accoutrements) is elaborated through slavery' (Wilderson 2020, 102), that is, a position structured outside of the self-possessed 'Human'. As Bliss writes: '"Antiblackness" names the *energy*, or the activity, of Humanity as a social structure. It does not simply name various forms of violence experienced by Blacks, but the violence that *positions* sentient beings outside the realm of the Human' (2015, 89 italics in original).

Black nihilism articulates 'hope against hope' as a 'necessary philosophical posture capable of unravelling the Political and its devastating logic of political hope' (Warren 2015, 7) in ways that extend to alternative ethicopolitical practices informed by hope, articulated as acting outside and otherwise to liberal modernist assumptions. The problem is the world itself, which is why Wilderson argues that what the Black demands is not freedom *within* the world but 'freedom *from* the world' (cited in Palmer 2020, 260 italics in original). As Tryone Palmer writes: 'The insistent attachment to the World, against the desire for its destruction, is a further retrenchment and reproduction of the violence of anti-Black modernity through the continued allegiance to World(ing) as generativity' (2020, 269).

Black nihilism and Afropessimism argue that the alternative to dominant approaches to hope and the ethicopolitical is the position of political apostasy, to 'reject the politics of hope' (Warren 2015, 8). Alternative approaches to the political, which draw upon hope, from this perspective, fail to adequately recognise the disastrousness of the world in their attempt to legitimise holding open otherwise worlds as a solution. This is a solution which is never open to critique as it is placed in the future, in the 'not yet' or the 'to come'. As Warren argues, in doing so: 'The politics of hope must actively refuse the possibility that the "solution" is, in fact, another problem in disguised form; the idea of a "solution" is nothing more than the repetition and disavowal of the problem itself' (2015, 11). Black nihilism therefore rejects 'the lure of emancipatory solutions', refusing politics and rejecting the reduction of possibilities to *this* world and its reproduction. This refusal, this political apostasy, 'is the only hope for blackness in an anti-black world' (Warren 2015, 12). Thus, Black nihilism does not seek to draw upon hope in order to articulate an alternative approach to the political but instead hopes 'for the end of political hope' (Warren 2015, 32).

CONCLUSION

Hope's ontological ambiguity has been put at the centre of this chapter. In engaging with this question, it becomes clear that the problem is one of ontological clarity. As Marcuse argued, it is the lack of attention to ontology that enables ethicopolitical imaginaries to displace political critique with moralism and conflates resignation and resistance. If *this* world is not enough and has never been enough, then working to reimagine it in terms of potential plenitude is merely to reproduce the world as it exists. These modes of deploying hope are therefore problematic because they cannot avoid the disavowal of the disastrousness that is constitutive of, and necessary for the reproduction of, *this* world. This inability is ontological, in that ethicopolitical projects that enrol hope necessarily either work as apologia ('optimism') or as disavowal ('utopianism').

For advocates of 'hope against hope' the problem of alternatives to the liberal political imaginary, informed by hope, is that they work in ways that similarly suborn individuals and communities to the reproduction of the system of repression. Of course, as analysed here, there are different inflections and approaches, but they problematise the use of hope to underpin projects that continue to reproduce assumptions of alternative futures at the expense of recognition of the disastrousness of this world. Adorno and Benjamin did much to lay the basis for 'hope against hope'. Adorno, for example, in warning that the disavowal of foundational and ongoing violence is a lure that should be rejected, arguing:

> One wants to break free of the past: rightly because nothing at all can live in its shadow, and because there will be no end to the terror as long as guilt and violence are repaid with guilt and violence; wrongly, because the past that one would like to evade is still very much alive.
>
> (cited in Winters 2016, 249)

Hope against hope is therefore very much in line with Walter Benjamin's attempt to articulate a hope that does not disavow the catastrophic impacts of colonial and capitalist modernity. Eagleton's (disapproving) reading draws out well Benjamin's focus on the ongoing violence which is disavowed by hope's enlistment into ethicopolitical projects (2017, 31–34). Benjamin's 'angel of history' sums this up well:

> His face is turned towards the past. Where we perceive a chain of events, he sees one single catastrophe which keeps piling wreckage upon wreckage and hurls it in

> front of his feet. The angel would like to stay, awaken the dead, and make whole what has been smashed. But a storm is blowing from Paradise; it has caught in his wings with such violence that the angel can no longer close them. This storm irresistibly propels him into the future to which his back his turned, while the pile of debris before him grows skyward. This storm is what we call progress.
>
> (Benjamin 2015b, 249)

Where liberal political imaginaries see progress and critical ethicopolitical imaginaries see futures of open-ended possibility, Benjamin's angel of history can only see the past in which one disaster follows another. This is a world of unending violence where 'there is no document of civilization which is not at the same time a document of barbarism' (2015b, 248). Eagleton calls Benjamin's a 'tragic form of hope' (2017, 33) and argues that: 'In Benjamin's view, the Kantian prospect of infinite progress is an image of Hell' (Eagleton 2017, 34). Here then, there is an understanding of how hegemonic political understandings require the disavowal of the reality of the world and that it is this disavowal that enables hope's enrolment in alternative ethicopolitical imaginaries of alternative futures. Where the negative ontological work in critical Crip, Indigenous, Queer and Black studies perhaps develops upon Benjamin's powerful historicist critique is in highlighting its ontological world constituting nature. Hope against hope therefore initiates the vital work of deconstructing hope's enablement of alternative ethicopolitical imaginaries, dependent upon this violence and its disavowal.

NOTES

1 Today, it appears, it is much more difficult to problematise hope's enrolment in the occlusion of the stakes involved in making a distinction between *this* world and any potential future one. One example of the contemporary appeal of this

conflation is Ida Danewid's award winning book, *Resisting Racial Capitalism* (2024). Drawing upon the Black radical tradition, particularly Robinson's *Black Marxism* and Kelley's *Freedom Dreams*, Danewid advocates an 'antipolitics of refusal', articulated 'as a project of building autonomy, care, and horizontalism beyond racial capitalism, the state, and their violent terms of order' (2024, 20); however, the book trades on ontological ambiguity in its articulation of a 'beyond' always in process, operating to elide the present with the future. It should be noted that the problem of ontological ambiguity is also central to other critical formulations of deconstruction. For a problematisation of readings of Derrida's conception of justice 'to come' in the discipline of International Relations see Chipato and Chandler (2024b).

2 William David Hart argues that this work is 'paradigm shifting' (2020, 4).

3 It should be noted that not all work that focuses on ontological questions necessarily fits with the discussion of 'hope against hope' as articulated in this section; see, for example, the 'black optimism' of Fred Moten (discussed in Chapter 1).

4 Wilderson argues that without Blacks:

> Humanity would cease to exist; because it would lose its conceptual coherence, having lost its baseline other. Humanity would find itself standing in the abyss of an epistemological void. The Black is needed to mark the border of Human subjectivity.
>
> (Wilderson 2020, 164)

CONCLUSION

INTRODUCTION

Hope is seen as enabling a range of important attempts to move beyond the limitations of traditional modernist modes of political understanding. The appeal of hope is perhaps stronger today than at any time previously. This appeal lies in the desire to keep alternative futures open in the face of the multiple closures of our broken worlds and the loss of attachment to traditional political institutional frameworks as the locus of transformative practices. Today, when hope is increasingly seen as enabling alternatives to formal political and policy framings, it is particularly important to highlight its problematic 'ambiguities' and to draw attention to the important work that lays a basis for disrupting and problematising hope's mainstreaming (the critical work analysed in the last chapter 'Hope against Hope').

At the centre of hope's utilisation within ethicopolitical alternatives has been a critical reworking of the understanding of the human, as the open-ended grounding of possibilities rather than a fixed and abstract liberal subject. Ethicopolitical praxes informed by hope project the human into an infinite or unknown future based on the human potential to become in excess of any framework of regulatory or governmental capture. As analysed above, this potentiality has been expressed in a number of different ways. This book has focused upon three interconnected modes through which hope has been enrolled in approaches which construct the human as exorbitant or excessive: through a focus upon libidinal drives, associated with nature or life itself; a focus upon the power of the human mind or the imagination and aesthetic propensities to break or rupture the hold of regimes of representation and, finally, human capacities for adaptation and resilience, becoming-with others in relational co-dependencies that enable multiple worlds of differentiated possibility.

In fine, critical attempts to hold open the possibility of alternative futures have utilised hope as a remaining resource in the wake of broken worlds, and in this way have posited a challenge to the liberal political order, making a number of ontological assumptions about the problems of this order and the 'human' that grounds it. The subject of ethicopolitical praxes informed by hope is a relational subject, a subject in its becoming, a subject that has no finalised or fixed identity but one in 'flight', in process. The human is always a project in process, always becoming; therefore, hope enables both utopian imaginaries of infinite futurity and optimistic imaginaries of resilient survivance. These (post)humanist promises of hope have been problematised in a number of ways, particularly in the framings discussed in the previous chapter 'Hope against Hope'. However, the purpose of this book has not been merely to survey ways in which hope has been enrolled to underpin alternative approaches to liberal modes of political engagement. It is important to highlight that this is merely the tip of the iceberg: hope was always implicit within the modern imaginary and today has assumed increasing importance in underpinning a much broader critical imaginary that far exceeds discussions directly concerning hope and futurity.

Critical thought has increasingly turned to hope in the struggle to hold open alternative futures. Without hope it would be necessary to confront the disastrousness of the world rather than seek to evade or disavow it. To make this point, this short concluding chapter, firstly seeks to highlight the limits of much of the critical work on the governmentalisation of hope. It suggests that this, predominantly Foucauldian, problematisation fails to engage more broadly with hope's ontological limitations. The biopolitical critique relies on hope being instrumentalised as a tool of power, designed to responsibilise and essentialise modes of coping and survivance. This book has sought to move beyond this critique and to problematise the utilisation of hope in ethicopolitical approaches and their ontology of world-making, self-making, plenitude and excess. In doing so, this concluding chapter engages with Marc Augé's *The Future* (2014) to emphasise the centrality of humanism to hope and closes with an extended reading of Louise Amoore's *Cloud Ethics* (2020) where the exorbitance of the human and the plenitude of the world beyond appearances necessarily provides the unacknowledged hope which implicitly underpins both critique and futural governing imaginaries today.

AFTER BIOPOLITICAL CRITIQUE

Alternative ethicopolitical approaches informed by hope have been central to the critical struggles of subaltern and marginalised groups isolated or excluded from traditional institutions of organised labour, through the 'Black Marxism' of C.L.R. James' radical workerism (Robinson 2000; Muñoz 2019),[1] the Black radical tradition, and up to contemporary critical and social theory, associated with critical Queer, Crip, Indigenous and Black studies. As this book has outlined, hope has been crucial to the understandings of alternative modes of ethicopolitical praxis which have undergone a transition from a material critique of the world, the world of racial capitalism, the world of oppression, and the denial of rights and equality, to an emphasis on 'worlding'. In this transition from 'world' to 'worlding', as Rizvana Bradley notes (2023), the identity construction of alternative 'subject' positions has consistently been eroded as the focus of hope has assumed an increasingly open-ended and futural register (see also Chipato and Chandler 2024b). Today the libidinal, life-driven, projects of hope (focused upon in Chapter 1) appear emptied of content. When hope has become virtual, without a subject, degraded of any radical potential, then, this book suggests, the ontological ambiguity of hope strategically serves the interests of power rather than resistance.

Today, the libidinal, aesthetic and relational drives of the human as subject have become the last refuges of governmentality; the points of access that are alleged to makes societies legible and to provide a field of governance. Hope informs alternative political imaginaries that enable and cohere governmental drives to govern through the removal of both 'inner' and 'outer' forms of repression or blockage. The problems of governance remain the same, but policy solutions are recast in terms of 'openness', 'response-ability' and adaptation (Chipato and Chandler 2024a). The libidinal drive, the eros, the desire that always says that the world is never everything, comes to the fore in the difficulty of articulating governance through positive goals and aspirations. Thus, hope enables the staging of an inversion whereby those least recognised or accepted in a modernist canon become fêted today. However, this is not necessarily a celebration of life as resistance or a crude romanticisation or essentialisation of those on the margins. It is important to challenge some of the critical assumptions of those who see in contemporary framings of hope merely the hand of hegemonic interests and reworking of modernist forms of control (for example, Evans and Reid 2014; Lindroth and Sinevaara-Niskanen 2022).

Firstly, for Foucauldian critics, the focus upon the struggles for survival of communities that are marginalised and excluded – the 'wretched', the 'damned' and the 'uninsured' dwellers of the 'borderlands' – is often problematised as a neoliberal governmentality. The seeming fêting of the subaltern is dismissed for essentialising modes of survivance, responsibilising marginal communities for worlding their worlds more efficiently, and forwarding new agendas of intervention and governance based on community enablement, resilience, and capacity-building (Huffer 2015; Lemke 2015). This critique however tends to miss some of the context. There has been a shift in the approach to the subaltern and to struggle such that today's marginal modes of survivance are not necessarily promoted as 'solutions' or as role models to be emulated in ways that they may have been in the early 2000s.[2] The appreciation of open-endedness, of the inaccessibility of the world, of alterity in itself, is increasingly becoming the point. Adaptive life is creative and differentiating, but there are not necessarily lessons to be learnt directly or indirectly, merely the adaptive need to move beyond rigid patterns of thought, to unthink or to unlearn accepted truths.

Fungi may have 36,000 sexes to assist in the process of adaptive differentiation but that does not mean that humans can or should emulate them (*Independent* 1999). However, it is held that knowing more about the sex life of fungi may help challenge accepted onto-epistemological understandings (de la Cadena 2022, 178). It is for this reason that more-than-human or non-human interlocutors are held to play a liberatory role, enabling the questioning and rethinking of accepted truths and possibilities to 'more creatively and generously hold open room in the world for others' (van Dooren 2022, 182). The task of hope today is more likely to be seen as one of holding open processes of thinking, imagining and of becoming rather than the urgent drive to replace one form of closure (Marxism, for example) with another, such as a dubious appeal 'to nature' (see van Dooren 2022, 186); or to 'what the Planet is telling us' (see Chandler et al 2018).

This shift, articulated in the language of Adorno, is one in which: 'The formal gesture of autonomy replaces the content of autonomy' (2003, 13). It is hard to argue against Adorno's problematisation of the subject- or agency-centred problematic, so central to ethicopolitical discourses underpinned by hope. In fact, aesthetic critiques and practices increasingly work upon the subject as the source of alternative futures. However, rather than aesthetics working to free or enable the subject's unconscious desires, critical theorists are much more likely to argue that even the unconscious is problematic and requires 'decolonising' (see, for example, Manchado de Oliviera 2021, 239). This is especially the case when it is considered that the shift, from conceiving the subject as separate from the world to realising the extent to which subjects are embedded within relations of becoming, may be deeply discomforting for the Western mind (Todd 2015; Kapoor 2014; Schomerus 2023). As Vanessa Andreotti argues: 'The irony is that the neutrality and universality at the core of this Cartesian subjectivity sustains the illusion of its unlimited capacity to know and apprehend reality, while hiding, precisely, how this capacity is severely limited' (Andreotti 2016, 104). The hold of modernity over even the subject's unconscious means that problems in the world are increasingly articulated in terms of the barrier of the subject's (imagination of) autonomy rather than in terms of the world as given, as a constraint.

Secondly, there has been a critique of the ideology of 'becoming-with', of overly affirmative imaginaries of new more-than-human, 'post-human', or multi-species collaboration. Axelle Karera highlights that the Anthropocene discourse of relational entanglement naturalises mutual processes of harmonious becoming, fetishising an apolitical understanding of 'life' (2019, 34). This critique is built upon by Dixa Ramirez D'Oleo (2023, 13) who powerfully argues that these discourses continue to disavow the destruction of others (see also Colebrook 2023). While there are some discourses of multi-species becoming that posit mutuality and harmony (Banerjee and Wouters 2022; Burke et al 2016), critical discourses increasingly draw upon hope while understanding that the process of open-ended becoming is one that is contested and at times violent (Bird Rose 2011). Today, struggles to hold open alternative futures tend to promise merely that the world can become otherwise not that there is some possibility of policy closure or a magical solution. Speculations of imminent harmony and perfection would be seen as 'abstract' or naïve ways of enrolling hope rather than as grounding feasible alternatives to linear and solution-based imaginaries.[3]

This book has argued that hope is certainly governmentalised but neither with the confidence of neoliberalism nor with the affirmation of some earlier discourses of multispecies becoming and 'more-than-human' assemblage. If anything, framings of hope register the exhaustion and closures of life's potentiality in the Anthropocene. To paraphrase Bruno Latour (2004), it is 'life' not only 'critique' that has 'run out of steam'. This is hardly surprising as the libidinal or negentropic power of life and the liberal political imaginary do not operate in a zero-sum relationship. Just as the human has revealed its exhaustion as an agential subject, so life too inevitably loses its vibrancy. The Anthropocene is then witness not to life's speciation and becoming but to its inability to adapt and to individuate in the face of global warming and catastrophic climate change. The biopolitical age appears to be ending, the libidinal drive is flagging, as Baudrillard states, the orgy has exhausted itself (1983). Without a confident or futural imaginary of the subject, hope has paradoxically become more central to contemporary thought but at the same time has retreated into the metaphysical realm, as an unquestioned assumption of critical ethicopolitical approaches, rather than as something to be openly theorised. It is for these reasons that the contemporary ways in which hope is utilised and the stakes involved need to be brought to the fore.

THE FUTURE

Marc Augé's *The Future* (2014) is a good starting place for highlighting the unacknowledged assumptions of alternative ethicopolitical imaginaries underpinned by hope. For Augé, the exhaustion of hope in formal political state-based institutional practice is clear as the modernist grand narrative of progress comes to an end (2014, 14). He argues that: 'The concept of governance proclaims the end of history... We are becoming used to the idea or image of a world without history or future, a world that has arrived, a finished world whose space is closing in on itself for good' (Augé 2014, 51, 42). The task then is to keep the future open, but this can only be done on the basis of hope, upon the assumption (we are now familiar with) that *this* world is never all that there is.

Of course, Augé does not seek to reproduce a Christian, a Marxist, or a psychoanalytical teleology of clear goals that give coherence to the world and to project this into the future. To hold open the future means to problematise and to ask questions of the present and to challenge deterministic assumptions. This open-endedness, required to keep the future open, can only come from an imaginary of the human as voluntaristically capable of shaping its own ends. For Augé, hope necessarily underpins this imaginary of the human and its capacities for learning and adaptation, its capacities for autonomous self-making that enable goals to emerge processually rather than operating in a linear manner with a fixed telos. The key point where hope comes in, to enable this praxis of holding alternative futures open in the face of broken worlds, is: '...the conviction – shared by all scientists - that the human mind has the capacity to make indefinite progress in learning, including knowledge of the cerebral mechanisms making this progress possible' (2014, 87).

For the human to play this role of enabling an open-ended futurity based on the adaptive and learning capacities of the human mind – something that apparently 'all scientists' agree with – something else is required. The other aspect required for hope as an alternative mode of ethicopolitical praxis that enables the futural imaginary is the promise of an accessible and universal world, a 'reality' that lies in excess of human knowledge and learning thus far. Hope thereby is fundamental for enabling alternative ethicopolitical imaginaries to critique the reductionist and abstract imaginaries of liberal modernity that assume that the future will be an extension of the past or that there is a coherent story of progress. Nevertheless, the metaphysical and ontological assumptions that ground a modernist imaginary are still present. The core unquestioned assumptions, essential to hope's utilisation for alternative ethicopolitical imaginaries, are that the human has immanent, hidden, repressed, capacities that can be 'freed' or enabled, and that human futurity, the 'indefinite' or the 'infinite' human 'to come', can be worlded in a world that is equally, constitutively, open in its becoming, providing a 'reality' beyond that grasped by contemporary modes of understanding.

ALGORITHMS AND THE HUMAN

Augé's *The Future* (2014) necessarily relies upon hope to underpin the processual open-ended praxis of becoming otherwise but it is clearly grounded in *this* world, in this world of the human as political subject and the world as an objective 'reality' beyond its grasp. The assumptions being made are overt if unquestioned. It is perhaps more important to critically engage with the utilisation of hope when it operates as the unquestioned ground not of liberal governing imaginaries of repair but of critical approaches, where the ostensible subject matter is not speculative futures but the critique of the ontological and epistemological closures imposed by regimes in the present. It is for this reason that this book closes with a critical reading of Louise Amoore's well-cited and well-respected book *Cloud Ethics: Algorithms and the Attributes of Ourselves and Others* (2020). I have selected this book as an exemplary example of contemporary critique, seeking to go beyond and to deconstruct a modernist political ontology. The engagement with the book is a purely heuristic one, to draw out how hope is enrolled implicitly to hold the future open and to cohere a 'future possibility for politics', beyond liberal constructions of the political (2020, 172).

Amoore's book is a powerful deconstruction of the processes of algorithmic decision-making as an example of modernist political reasoning. She draws upon the critical resources of continental philosophy, upon the work of Foucault, Deleuze and Derrida, as well as the critical scientific feminist approaches of Karen Barad and Donna Haraway, to problematise the operation of algorithms and the world they construct and seek to predict and govern. Key to the argumentation of the book is that machine-learning algorithms develop as iterative and relational apparatuses no longer determined by their initial source code; however, accountability is not the only problem. The ethical questions algorithms raise are not new but go to the heart of a modern ontology that presupposes a world of transparency, a world available to be known, categorised and thereby regulated. Thus, the algorithm is not itself the problem but rather the modernist assumptions that underpin their use and the understanding that their decision-making can be somehow an objective reflection of reality. Like any process of decision-making, algorithms 'condense multiple potential futures into a single output' (2020, 4).

Against the certainties imagined to be generated through machine-learning algorithms, Amoore forwards an alternative ethicopolitical project of 'cloud ethics' which asserts that 'ethical responsibility is sustained by conditions of partiality and opacity' (2020, 8). Calling algorithms to account is not a matter of deterministically and reductively considering them in goal-directed cause-and-effect ways, in attempts to locate a human intentionality behind their outcomes. Rather, it is to trace the processes through which they construct the world as meaningful, via a series of propositions, patterns and cluster recognition, that enables cuts and categorisations that inevitably involve contingent and subjective weightings and biases. In short, the problem of algorithmic decision-making brings into sharp relief the broader problems of a liberal political ontology – an approach to the world that is necessarily reductionist of its multiplicity – that phenomenologically, perceptually, reduces the world to what is considered to be already important (the training data which is thereby necessarily incomplete).

'Whether someone or something can be recognized depends on what the algorithm has been exposed to in the world' (Amoore 2020, 73). It is for this reason that: 'At root, the algorithm can never be neutral or without bias or prejudice because it must have assumptions to extract from its environment, to adapt, and to learn' (Amoore 2020, 75). Algorithms, by their nature, cannot recognise singularity or particularity; they are trained only to recognise and adapt the thresholds between sets of differences and similarities in attributes of different data populations (2020, 101). Thus: 'A principle harm of algorithms is that they enable calculative action where there is incalculability and the unknowable, reducing ethicopolitical orientations to the optimization of outputs and resolution of difficulties' (Amoore 2020, 119). This violence is disavowed as the 'algorithm underwrites its own rationality because it is engaged in defining new thresholds of normal and abnormal behaviours, reasonable and unreasonable travel, the arbitration of the good and the bad' (Amoore 2020, 129).

In realising these shortcomings and their inevitable violence to the reality of the world, new possibilities are opened up 'onto a different kind of community and a different mode of being together, being ethicopolitical' (Amoore 2020, 25). A 'cloud ethics should proceed from the incompleteness and undecidability of all forms of decision' (Amoore 2020, 121). Rather than the certainty of these machinic cuts, Amoore's ethicopolitical alternative is to place doubt at the centre, in order to acknowledge the 'fullness and plenitude of other possible incalculable paths' (Amoore 2020, 142). Amoore's deconstructive methodology centres upon the inevitable excess of complex reality in relation to algorithmic machine learning's attempt to see and construct the world meaningfully. It is with the unseen and the 'unattributable' that hope and open-ended futurity are then held to lie (Amoore 2020, 158). Amoore's ontological critique identifies 'a profound violence in the algorithm's foreclosure of alternative futures' (Amoore 2020, 161):

> There is a political refusal in claiming the unattributable. It is a refusal to be governed by the attribute… My ethicopolitical relations to myself and to others, then, cannot be limited to recognizable attributes but must begin from a recognition of singularity.
>
> (Amoore 2020, 171)

Hope here is utilised to provide the grounds for Amoore's 'cloud ethics' and to inform an alternative mode of ethicopolitical praxis. While hope in modernist modes of representation and governance may be waning this example makes clear that hope itself – in providing the conceptual underpining for alternative modes of refusal and resistance to governing regimes of representation and repression – appears alive and well. The unquestioned assumptions are what are of interest here. As noted in the opening section of this chapter, on the lack of content of futural imaginaries, Amoore's ethicopolitical alternative has no transformatory ethos or promise; there is no biopolitical assumption of survivance or of responsibilising marginalised communities, nor are there any relational claims of adaptive co- and more-than-human becoming. Futural possibilities for politics are left open-ended and formal gestures towards alternative futures are expressed, where the common is constituted precisely through the excess or exorbitance to representation of the human as political subject:

> A cloud ethics must pursue a conception of being together as a society of the unattributable, where what we share in common is precisely our singularities... Ethicopolitical life is about irresolvable struggles, intransigence, duress, and opacity, and it must continue to be so if a future possibility for politics is not to be eclipsed by the output signals of algorithms.
>
> (Amoore 2020, 172)

Of course, this future human, the human beyond representation, beyond attribution, marked only by its excess, its exorbitance, its particularity, its singularity, is no less of an abstraction than the liberal autonomous, rights- and interests-bearing subject. The violence of the algorithm is a violence to a 'reality' conceived of as marked by the 'fullness and plenitude of other possible incalculable paths'; this 'profound violence' is to be found 'in the algorithm's foreclosure of alternative futures'. As argued in the closing chapters of this book, hope thereby is enrolled to necessarily constrict any room for calls for a recognition of, or for justice in the cause of, all those sacrificed at the altar of liberal modernity; there can be no recognition of the grounding violence that enables 'the human', if 'the world' is to be imagined with such 'plenitude' and 'possibility'.

'Hope against hope' suggests a challenge to the unexamined assumptions of hope that haunt ethicopolitical imaginaries which claim to be critical of a liberal political ontology of violent cuts and divisions. Any meaningful alternative to this world would need to critically examine the assumptions of 'ontological plenitude' (Chamberlin 2024, 183) that conflate today's world alienation with a future beyond this alienated condition. The problem with ethicopolitical assumptions, that are underpinned by hope for otherwise worlds in the ontological excess of *this* world, is their necessarily affirmative stance. This stance may be critical, but it coheres the modernist imaginary of a subject and world rather than problematising it. As Tryone Palmer has argued, this 'continued insistence on "another world"' functionally reproduces this one (2020, 250). Thus, hope is only for those who are secured by this world and affirmed in it, those who can world themselves unproblematically, at home in a world of antiblackness, in a world of alienation. The world of 'plenitude' and 'excess' is 'shockingly white', argues Palmer (2020, 254).

Thus, Amoore's critique of the 'profound violence' being done to 'alternative futures' (Amoore 2020, 161) is quite different to a 'hope against hope' critique, which would highlight the ongoing violence of the world itself, which makes any algorithmic source data equally tainted by the 'reality' of racial exclusion and social and economic division. Algorithms would then reproduce the violence of the world because the world is not a world of 'plenitude' and infinite 'incalculable paths' and because the future is not, in fact, 'open' to 'incalculable' otherwise possibilities but already profoundly limited by this foundational and ongoing structuring violence. In refusing Amoore's utilisation of hope to underpin the ethicopolitical practice of 'cloud ethics', we are forced to confront, rather than to disavow this reality.

CONCLUSION

It appears that hope is increasingly constitutive for ethicopolitical imaginaries with the multiple closures of this broken world. These closures extend well beyond catastrophic climate change, ongoing racial exclusion and international conflict, to include the exhaustion more broadly of the formal state-based politics of representation. In these approaches, hope is not placed in liberal modernist assumptions of the political subject, political reason and instrumentalised and goal-directed policy-making, but is utilised for a rejection of this liberal imaginary. Thus, there appear to be three ways in which hope is utilised today.

Firstly, there is what might be called the 'liberal' utilisation of hope, that is overtly focused upon the repair of *this* world. Liberal or modernist uses of hope take the form of moralised calls to action to save imaginaries of progress and social harmony, or they may also use hope in more mournful or melancholic ways, recognising the limits of modernist aspirations of political justice and social inclusion. This book has been less concerned with this approach to hope which is analysed in the Introduction chapter and has been extensively engaged with in analytical philosophy and social psychology.

Secondly, there is what might be called the 'critical' utilisations of hope; the use of hope to underpin alternative ethicopolitical approaches, critical of liberal modernist assumptions and separations. These approaches have been framed heuristically in this book through an analytical engagement with the ways in which hope has been utilised: the focus upon libidinal drives and desires; the importance of aesthetics as a field of contestation and enablement; and practices of becoming in relation. These alternatives prioritised an open-ended imaginary of the human and the world, full of untapped potentiality beyond the narrow reductionist categories and concerns of liberal thought.

In the final chapter, a third, more negative or nihilist form of 'hope against hope', or what might be called a 'post-critical' utilisation of hope, was brought to the fore. While still working in the extended critical tradition, in critical Black, Queer, Indigenous and Crip studies, there is a growing concern with ontological questions which problematise the generative assumptions of much of the earlier work in these areas. In the conclusion, this book has sought to underline the importance of 'hope against hope' not by repeating the arguments of the advocates of this approach but by highlighting the extent to which the modernist construction of the human still haunts critical approaches to the liberal political imaginary. Hope has been a fundamental underpinning for ethicopolitical alternatives that, as we have seen, continue to disavow the disastrousness of the world. This disavowal is necessary to imagine and to cohere 'a future possibility for politics'. Imaginaries of alternative futures and 'otherwise worlds', struggling within and against the closures of broken worlds, are thereby brought into question by more recent work in the critical tradition. Kant's third critical question, 'What may I hope?' thereby remains of central concern for anyone interested in confronting the multiple closures of our contemporary condition.

NOTES

1 It was James who coined the key trope, of alternative ethicopolitical projects informed by hope, of belief in 'the future in the present', in a letter to a friend in 1953 (Rachleff 1994).

2 Where there are still legacies of modernist political activism, the problem-solving claims can appear particularly contested, with a thin line often dividing community empowerment from 'neoliberal' forms of social control. See for example, Robin Kelley's endorsement of community projects, like the Detroit Black Community Food Security Network (DBCFSN), seen to work on both changing the world and the subject:

> ...to promote urban agriculture, healthy diets, cooperatives, environmental justice, sustainability, self-reliance and self-determination... Through its "Food Warriors" program, DBCFSN trains young people in the techniques of sustainable farming, encourages healthy lifestyles, and builds intergenerational community solidarity... It is largely a Black working-class movement to create a "new commons," a sustainable future, and a hedge against gentrification and dispossession.
>
> (Kelley 2022, 211)

If the world shrinks to the experiential level of the community, then worlding becomes a matter of transforming the individual rather than the world itself; a matter of survivance rather than of radical transformation. The process is rather one of adaptation and resilience: 'hedging against', rather than resisting, gentrification and dispossession.

3 See, for example, the range of critical responses, from Gayatri Chakravorty Spivak (2022), Marisol de la Cadena (2022) and Thom van Dooren (2022) to Milinda Banerjee and Jelle J.P. Wouters (2022) who claim that Indigenous communities offer generalisable policy solutions capable of solving the problems of climate change. Gayatri Chakravorty Spivak clarifies there can be no direct appropriation or application of what are assumed to be subaltern approaches (2022, 166–167). Marisol de la Cadena argues that conversation may be possible in 'pluriversal contact zones' but that 'modern audiences need to control to avoid colonial practices of equivocation' that would translate Indigenous concepts into modern relations of belief and being (de la Cadena 2022, 178; see also Spivak 2022, 167). Subaltern struggles or the Black radical tradition no longer provides direct resources that can be drawn upon but rather an indirect one, a differentiation that enables readers to rethink or to challenge their own assumptions of fixity or closure.

REFERENCES

Adorno, T. 2003 [1964]. *The Jargon of Authenticity*. Abingdon: Routledge.

Amoore, L. 2020. *Cloud Ethics: Algorithms and the Attributes of Ourselves and Others*. Durham, NC: Duke University Press.

Andreotti, V. 2016. The Educational Challenges of Imagining the World Differently. *Canadian Journal of Development Studies/ Revue canadienne d'études du développement* 37(1): 101–112.

Andriote, J.-M. 2024. Hope Is a Choice to Make Things Better. *Psychology Today*, 1 March. https://www.psychologytoday.com/gb/blog/stonewall-strong/202403/hope-is-a-choice-to-make-things-better.

Augé, M. 2014. *The Future*. London: Verso.

Banerjee, M. and Wouters, J. J. P. 2022. *Subaltern Studies 2.0*. Chicago, IL: Prickly Paradigm Press.

Bargués, P., Chandler, D., Schindler, S. and Waldow, V. 2024. Hope after 'the End of the world': Rethinking Critique in the Anthropocene. *Contemporary Political Theory* 23(3): 187–204.

Baudrillard, J. 1983. What Are You Doing after the Orgy? *Artforum* 22(2). https://www.artforum.com/features/what-are-you-doing-after-the-orgy-201860/.

Benedicto, B. 2019. Agents and Objects of Death: Gay Murder, Boyfriend Twins, and Queer of Color Negativity. *GLQ: A Journal of Lesbian and Gay Studies* 25(2): 273–296.

Benhabib, S. 1990. Critical Theory and Postmodernism: On the Interplay of Ethics, Aesthetics, and Utopia in Critical Theory. *Cardozo Law Review* 11: 1435–1448.

Benjamin, W. 2015a. Franz Kafka: On the Tenth Anniversary of His Death. In W. Benjamin, *Illuminations*. London: Bodley Head, 108–135.

Benjamin, W. 2015b. Theses on the Philosophy of History. In W. Benjamin, *Illuminations*. London: Bodley Head, 245–255.

Ben-Moshe, L. 2018. Dis-Epistemologies of Abolition. *Critical Criminology* 26(3): 341–355.

Bennett, J. 2010. *Vibrant Matter: A Political Ecology of Things*. Durham, NC: Duke University Press.

Beradi, F. B. 2011. *After The Future*. Edinburgh: AK Press.

Berlant, L. 2011. *Cruel Optimism*. Durham, NC: Duke University Press.

Bérubé, M. 2006. Introduction: Another World Is Possible. In R. McRuer, *Crip Theory: Cultural Signs of Queerness and Disability*. New York: New York University Press, vii–xi.

Bey, M. 2022. *Black Trans Feminism*. Durham, NC: Duke University Press.

Bird Rose, D. 2011. *Wild Dog Dreaming: Love and Extinction*. Charlottesville: University of Virginia Press.

Bleiker, R. 2001. The Aesthetic Turn in International Political Theory. *Millennium: Journal of International Studies* 30(3): 509–533.

Bleiker, R. 2017. In Search of Thinking Space: Reflections on the Aesthetic Turn in International Political Theory. *Millennium: Journal of International Studies* 45(2): 258–264.

Bliss, J. 2015. Hope Against Hope: Queer Negativity, Black Feminist Theorizing, and Reproduction Without Futurity. *Mosaic* 48(1): 83–98.

Bloch, E. 1986 [1959]. *The Principle of Hope Volume One*. Cambridge, MA: MIT Press.

Bloch, E. and Adorno, T. W. 1988. Something's Missing: A Discussion between Ernst Bloch and Theodor W. Adorno on the Contradictions of Utopian Longing. In E. Bloch, *The Utopian Function of Art and Literature: Selected Essays*. Cambridge, MA: MIT Press, 1–17.

Bosch, A. and Promberger, M. 2020. Aesthetics, Self-reliance and Resilience. In M. Boost, J. Dagg, J. Gray and M. Promberger (eds) *Poverty, Crisis and Resilience*. Cheltenham: Edward Elgar, 220–231.

Bradley, R. 2023. *Anteaesthetics: Black Aesthesis and the Critique of Form*. Stanford, CA: Stanford University Press.

Brigstocke, J. and Gassner, G. 2021. Materiality, Race, and Speculative Aesthetics. *GeoHumanities* 7(2): 359–369.

Brigstocke, J. and Noorani, T. 2016. Posthuman Attunements: Aesthetics, Authority and the Arts of Creative Listening. *GeoHumanities* 2(1): 1–7.

Burke, A., Fishel, S., Mitchell, A., Dalby, S. and Levine, D. J. 2016. Planet Politics: A Manifesto from the End of IR. *Millennium: Journal of International Studies* 44(3): 499–523.

Burke, E. 2015 [1757]. *Philosophical Enquiry into the Origin of Our Ideas of the Sublime and the Beautiful.* Oxford: Oxford University Press.

Burris, B. 2017. Birth of a (Zionist) Nation: Black Radicalism and the Future of Palestine. In G. T. Johnson and A. Lubin (eds) *Futures of Black Radicalism.* London: Verso, 120–132.

Chamberlin, C. 2024. What Is the Libidinal Economy of Antiblackness? In B. Gook (ed.) *Libidinal Economies of Crisis Times: The Psychic Life of Contemporary Capitalism.* Bielefeld: transcript Verlag, 177–194.

Chandler, D. 2013. Human-Centred' Development? Rethinking 'Freedom' and 'Agency' in Discourses of International Development. *Millennium: Journal of International Studies* 42(1): 3–23.

Chandler, D. 2018. *Ontopolitics in the Anthropocene: An Introduction to Mapping, Sensing and Hacking.* Abingdon: Routledge.

Chandler, D. 2024a. The Politics of the Unseen: Speculative, Pragmatic and Nihilist Hope in the Anthropocene. *Distinktion: Journal of Social Theory* 25(1): 1–18.

Chandler, D. 2024b. Development After the End of the World. *Civil Wars* 26(4): 733–736.

Chandler, D. 2025. 'Un-Cancelling the Future': Kantian Ethics and the Ukraine War. *New Perspectives* 33(3): 262–275.

Chandler, D., Cudworth, E. and Hobden, S. 2018. Anthropocene, Capitalocene and Liberal Cosmopolitan IR: A Response to Burke et al.'s 'Planet Politics. *Millennium: Journal of International Studies* 46(2): 190–208.

Chandler, D., Müller, F. and Rothe, D. 2021. *International Relations in the Anthropocene: New Agendas, New Agencies and New Approaches.* Basingstoke: Palgrave Macmillan.

Chandler, D. and Reid, J. 2019. *Becoming Indigenous: Governing Imaginaries in the Anthropocene.* London: Rowman & Littlefield.

Chibber, V. 2013. *Postcolonial Theory and the Spectre of Capital.* London: Verso.

Chignell, A. 2024. The Focus Theory of Hope. In N. E. Snow (ed.) *The Virtue of Hope*. Oxford: Oxford University Press, 109–138.

Chipato, F. 2024. The Aesthetics of Peace: Complexity, Speculation, and Unknowing in Creative Peacebuilding Research. *Journal of Intervention and Statebuilding* 18(3): 225–243.

Chipato, F. and Chandler, D. 2024a. *Race in the Anthropocene: Coloniality, Disavowal and the Black Horizon*. Abingdon: Routledge.

Chipato, F. and Chandler, D. 2024b. Justice "to Come"? Decolonial Deconstruction, from Postmodern Policymaking to the Black Horizon. *International Political Sociology* 18(4): olae041.

Colebrook, C. 2010. Toxic Feminism: Hope and Hopelessness after Feminism. *Journal for Cultural Research* 14(4): 323–335.

Colebrook, C. 2023. *Who Would You Kill to Save the World?* Lincoln, NE: University of Nebraska Press.

Connolly, W. E. 2011. *A World of Becoming*. Durham, NC: Duke University Press.

Connolly, W. E. 2013. *The Fragility of Things: Self-Organizing Processes, Neoliberal Fantasies, and Democratic Activism*. Durham, NC: Duke University Press.

Cravey, A. J. and Petit, M. 2018. Indigenous Moves: Collaborative Multimedia and Decolonial Aesthetics. *GeoHumanities* 4(2): 360–79.

Crawley, A. T. 2017. *Blackpentecostal Breath: The Aesthetics of Possibility*. New York: Fordham University Press.

Cuervo, H. and Cook, J. 2019. In Defence of Hope: Towards a Sociology of Hope in Crisis Times. *The Sociological Review*, 30 September. https://thesociologicalreview.org/collections/guest-essays/in-defence-of-hope/.

Danewid, I. 2024. *Resisting Racial Capitalism: An Antipolitical Theory of Refusal*. Cambridge: Cambridge University Press.

Danowski, D. and Viveiros de Castro, E. 2017. *The Ends of the World*. Cambridge: Polity.

Davidson, M. 2024. On the concept of the pluriverse in Walter Mignolo and the European New Right. *Contemporary Political Theory* online first 19 November.

Day, J. P. 1969. Hope. *American Philosophical Quarterly* 6(2): 89–102.

de la Cadena, M. 2022. The Gift of the Anthropo-Not-Seen: Pluriversal Contact Zones and Speech in Translation. In M. Banerjee and J. J. P. Wouters, *Subaltern Studies 2.0*. Chicago, IL: Prickly Paradigm Press, 169–179.

de la Cadena, M. and Blaser, M. eds. 2018. *A World of Many Worlds*. Durham, NC: Duke University Press.

Der Derian, J. and Wendt, A. eds. 2022. *Quantum International Relations: A Human Science for World Politics*. Oxford: Oxford University Press.

Donald, M. J. 2018. We Are Not Walking Wave Functions: A Response to 'Quantum Mind and Social Science' by Alexander Wendt. *Journal for the Theory of Social Behaviour* 48(2): 153–251.

Du Bois, W. E. B. 1998. [1935]. *Black Reconstruction in America 1860–1880*. New York: Free Press.

Du Bois, W. E. B. 2018. [1903]. *The Souls of Black Folk*. Amazon Kindle Direct Publishing.

Eagleton, T. 2017. *Hope Without Optimism*. New Haven, CT: Yale University Press.

Edelman, L. 2022. *Bad Education: Why Queer Theory Teaches Us Nothing*. Durham, NC: Duke University Press.

Edwards, L. M. and McConnell, K. R. 2024. The Influence of Culture on Psychological Hope. In N. E. Snow (ed.) *The Virtue of Hope*. Oxford: Oxford University Press, 227–251.

Escobar, A. 2017. *Designs for the Pluriverse: Radical Interdependence, Autonomy, and the Making of Worlds*. Durham, NC: Duke University Press.

Evans, B. and Reid, J. 2014. *Resilient Life: The Art of Living Dangerously*. Cambridge: Polity.

Fanon, F. 1986. [1952]. *Black Skin, White Masks*. London: Pluto Press.

Featherstone, M. 2002. Empire and Utopia: A Psychoanalytic Critique of Totality. *Cultural Values* 6(4): 369–384.

Ferdinand, M. 2022. *Decolonial Ecology: Thinking from the Caribbean World*. Cambridge: Polity Press.

Fisher, M. 2014. *Capitalist Realism: Is There an Alternative?* Winchester: Zero Books.

Fontanari, E. 2019. *Lives in Transit: An Ethnographic Study of Refugees' Subjectivity Across European Borders*. Abingdon: Routledge.

Frost, L. 2010. Aesthetics and Politics. *Global Society* 24(3): 433–443.

Gäckle, N. 2024. Enduring Hopelessness: Governance Without Horizon in Pandemic Times. In Waldow, V., Bargués, P. and Chandler, D. (eds.) *Hope in the Anthropocene: Agency, Governance and Negation*. Edinburgh: Edinburgh University Press, 103–118.

Gaztambide-Fernández, R. 2014. Decolonial Options and Artistic/AestheSic Entanglements: An Interview With Walter Mignolo. *Decolonization: Indigeneity, Education & Society* 3(1): 196–212.

Gilmore, R. W. 2017. Abolition Geography and the Problem of Innocence. In G. T. Johnson and A. Lubin (eds) *Futures of Black Radicalism*. London: Verso, 225–240.

Gilmore, R. W. 2022. *Abolition Geography: Essays Towards Liberation*. London: Verso.

Gordon, A. F. 2019. Preface. In (eds) *An Anthropology of Marxism*. London: Pluto Press, xiii–xxix.

Gordon, L. R. 2024. A Black Existential Reflection on Hope. In N. E. Snow (ed.) *The Virtue of Hope*. Oxford: Oxford University Press, 139–161.

Gravlin, M. 2024. Prophecy Redux: A Critique of Leanne Simpson's Concept of Autogenocide. *Settler Colonial Studies* Online First 2 October.

Grove, J. 2019. *Savage Ecology: War and Geopolitics at the End of the World*. Durham, NC: Duke University Press.

Grove, K. 2018. *Resilience*. Abingdon: Routledge.

Grove, K. and Adey, P. 2015. Security and the Politics of Resilience: An Aesthetic Response. *Politics* 35(1): 78–84.

Gulliford, L. 2024. Hope: An Interdisciplinary Examination. In N. E. Snow (ed.) *The Virtue of Hope*. Oxford: Oxford University Press, 201–225.

Gumbs, A. P. 2020. *Undrowned: Black Feminist Lessons from Marine Animals*. Chico, CA: AK Press.

Hage, G. 2009. Waiting Out the Crisis: On Stuckedness and Governmentality. In G. Hage (ed.) *Waiting Out the Crisis: On Stuckedness and Governmentality*. Melbourne: Melbourne University Press, 1–9.

Han-Pile, B. and Stern, R. 2024. Is Hope a Secular Virtue? Hope as the Virtue of the Possible. In N. E. Snow (ed.) *The Virtue of Hope*. Oxford: Oxford University Press, 73–108.

Haraway, D. 2016. *Staying With the Trouble: Making Kin in the Chthulucene*. Durham, NC: Duke University Press.

Hardt, M. and Negri, A. 2000. *Empire*. Cambridge, MA: Harvard University Press.

Harney, S. and Moten, F. 2013. *The Undercommons: Fugitive Planning & Black Study*. New York: Minor Compositions.

Harney, S. and Moten, F. 2021. *All Incomplete*. New York: Minor Compositions.

Hart, W. D. 2020. *The Blackness of Black: Key Concepts in Critical Discourse*. Lanham, MA: Lexington Books.

Hartman, S. V. 1997. *Scenes of Subjection: Terror, Slavery, and Self-Making in Nineteenth-Century America*. Oxford: Oxford University Press.

Hawkins, H. 2025. Cultural geographies III: What if...? Imagination, Worldly Relations and doing Research Otherwise. *Progress in Human Geography* Online First DOI: 10.1177/03091325251320247.

Herz, M., Lalander, P. and Elsrud, T. 2022. Governing Through Hope: An Exploration of Hope and Social Change in an Asylum Context. *Emotions and Society* 4(2): 222–237.

Hine, D. 2023. *At Work in the Ruins: Finding Our Place in the Time of Science Climate Change Pandemics & All the Other Emergencies*. London: Chelsea Green Publishing.

Huffer, L. 2015. Foucault's Fossils: Life Itself and the Return to Nature in Feminist Philosophy. *Foucault Studies* 20: 122–141.

Hui, Y. 2015. Modulation after control. *New Formations* 84/85: 74–91.

Hui, Y. 2021. *Art and Cosmotechnics*. Minneapolis, MN: University of Minnesota Press.

Husserl, E. 1970 [1954] *The Crisis of the European Sciences and Transcendental Phenomenology: An Introduction to Phenomenological Philosophy*. Evanston, IL: Northwestern University Press.

Hutcheson, S. 2025. The Power of Hope: A Pathway to Resilience and Positive Growth. *Forbes*, 13 January. https://www.forbes.com/sites/scotthutcheson/2025/01/13/the-power-of-hope-a-pathway-to-resilience-and-positive-growth/.

Independent. 1999. Scientists Discover Why Fungi Have 36,000 Sexes. *Independent* 15 September. https://www.independent.co.uk/news/scientists-discover-why-fungi-have-36-000-sexes-1119181.html#.

Jackson, M. 2016. Aesthetics, Politics. Attunement: On Some Questions Brought by Alterity and Ontology. *GeoHumanities* 2(1): 8–23.

Kafer, A. 2013. *Feminist, Queer, Crip*. Bloomington, IN: Indiana University Press.

Kallio, K. P., Meier, I. and Häkli, J. 2021. Radical Hope in Asylum Seeking: Political Agency Beyond Linear Temporality. *Journal of Ethnic and Migration Studies* 47(17): 4006–4022.

Kant, I. 1970 [1795]. Perpetual Peace: A Philosophical Sketch. In: H. S. Reiss (ed.) *Kant: Political Writings*. Cambridge: Cambridge University Press, 93–130.

Kant, I. 2002 [1790]. *The Critique of the Power of Judgement*. Cambridge: Cambridge University Press.

Kapoor, I. 2014. Psychoanalysis and Development: Contributions, Examples, Limits. *Third World Quarterly* 35(7): 1120–1143.

Karera, A. 2019. Blackness and the Pitfalls of Anthropocene Ethics. *Critical Philosophy of Race* 7(1): 32–56.

Kelley, R. D. G. 2022. *Freedom Dreams: The Black Radical Imagination*. Boston, MA: Beacon Press.

Kimmerer, R. W. 2015. *Braiding Sweetgrass: Indigenous Wisdom, Scientific Knowledge and the Teachings of Plants*. Minneapolis, MN: Milkweed Editions.

King, T. L., Navarro, J. and Smith, A. eds. 2020. *Otherwise Worlds: Against Settler Colonialism and Anti-Blackness*. Durham, NC: Duke University Press.

Koddenbrock, K. J. 2014. Strategies of Critique in International Relations: From Foucault and Latour Towards Marx. *European Journal of International Relations* 21(2): 243–266.

Lamb, M. 2024. Difficult Hope: Wendell Berry and Climate Change. In N. E. Snow (ed.) *The Virtue of Hope*. Oxford: Oxford University Press, 345–379.

Latour, B. 2004. Why Has Critique Run Out of Steam? From Matters of Fact to Matters of Concern. *Critical Inquiry* 30(2): 225–248.

Latour, B. 2018. *Down to Earth: Politics in the New Climatic Regime*. Cambridge: Polity Press.

Latour, B., Stengers, I., Tsing, A. and Bubandt, N. 2018. Anthropologists Are Talking – About Capitalism, Ecology, and Apocalypse. *Ethnos* 83(3): 587–606.

Law, J. 2015. What's Wrong With a One-World World? *Distinktion: Journal of Social Theory* 16(1): 126–139.

Lear, J. 2008. *Radical Hope: Ethics in the Face of Cultural Devastation*. Cambridge, MA: Harvard University Press.

Lemke, T. 2015. New Materialisms: Foucault and the 'Government of Things. *Theory, Culture & Society* 32(4): 3–25.

Lemke, T. 2021. *The Government of Things: Foucault and the New Materialisms*. New York: New York University Press.
Lindroth, M. and Sinevaara-Niskanen, H. 2022. *The Colonial Politics of Hope: Critical Junctures of Indigenous-State Relations*. Abingdon: Routledge.
Lipsitz, G. 2017. What Is This Black in the Black Radical Tradition. In G. T. Johnson and A. Lubin (eds) *Futures of Black Radicalism*. London: Verso, 108–119.
Lloyd, D. 2019. *Under Representation: The Racial Regime of Aesthetics*. New York: Fordham University Press.
Lyotard, J.-F. 2004 [1974]. *Libidinal Economy*. London: Bloomsbury.
Manchado de Oliviera, V. 2021. *Hospicing Modernity: Facing Humanity's Wrongs and the Implications for Social Activism*. Berkeley, CA: North Atlantic Books.
Marcuse, H. 1987. [1956] *Eros and Civilization: A Philosophical Inquiry into Freud*. London: ARK.
Marriott, D. 2000. *On Black Men*. Edinburgh: Edinburgh University Press.
Martineau, J. and Ritskes, E. 2014. Fugitive Indigeneity: Reclaiming the Terrain of Decolonial Struggle Through Indigenous Art. *Decolonization: Indigeneity, Education & Society* 3(1): I–XII.
Mbembe, A. 2017. *Critique of Black Reason*. Durham, NC: Duke University Press.
McRuer, R. 2006. *Crip Theory: Cultural Signs of Queerness and Disability*. New York: New York University Press.
Mignolo, W. D. 2018a. On Pluriversality and Multipolar World Order: Decoloniality after Decolonization; Dewesternization after the Cold War. In B. Reiter (ed.) *Constructing the Pluriverse*. Durham, NC: Duke University Press, 90–116.
Mignolo, W. D. 2018b. Decoloniality and Phenomenology: The Geopolitics of Knowing and Epistemic/Ontological Colonial Differences. *The Journal of Speculative Philosophy* 32(3): 360–387.
Mignolo, W. D. and Vazquez, R. 2013. Decolonial AestheSis: Colonial Wounds/Decolonial Healings. *Social Text* Online 15. https://socialtextjournal.org/periscope_article/decolonial-aesthesis-colonial-woundsdecolonial-healings/
Mika, C., Andreotti, V., Cooper, G., Ahenakew, C. and Silva, D. F. 2020. The Ontological Differences between Wording and Worlding the World. *Language, Discourse & Society* 8(1): 17–32.
Moten, F. 2008. The Case of Blackness. *Criticism* 50(2): 177–218.

Moten, F. 2013. Blackness and Nothingness (Mysticism in the Flesh). *The South Atlantic Quarterly* 112(4): 737–780.

Muñoz, J. E. 2019 [2009]. *Cruising Utopia, 10th Anniversary Edition: The Then and There of Queer Futurity.* New York: New York University Press.

Negri, A. 1999. *Insurgencies: Constituent Power and the Modern State.* Minneapolis: University of Minnesota Press.

Nietzsche, F. 2004. *Human, All Too Human.* London: Penguin Books.

Obama, B. 2008. *The Audacity of Hope: Thoughts on Reclaiming the American Dream.* Edinburgh: Canongate Books.

Oettingen, G. 2024. Positive Fantasies About the Future Breed Hope. In N. E. Snow (ed.) *The Virtue of Hope.* Oxford: Oxford University Press, 253–275.

Palmer, T. S. 2020. Otherwise than Blackness: Feeling, World, Sublimation. *Qui Parle* 29(2): 247–283.

Potkay, A. 2024. Virtue or Vice? A Short Literary History of Hope. In N. E. Snow (ed.) *The Virtue of Hope.* Oxford: Oxford University Press, 47–71.

Povinelli, E. 2021. *Between Gaia and Ground: Four Axioms of Existence and the Ancestral Catastrophe of Late Liberalism.* Durham, NC: Duke University Press.

Puar, J. K. 2017. *The Right to Maim: Debility, Capacity, Disability.* Durham, NC: Duke University Press.

Quan, H. L. T. 2017. "It's Hard to Stop Rebels That Time Travel": Democratic Living and the Radical Reimaging of Old Worlds. In G. T. Johnson and A. Lubin (eds) *Futures of Black Radicalism.* London: Verso, 173–193.

Rachleff, P. 1994. The Future Is in the Present. *Monthly Review* 45(10): 52–57. https://monthlyreviewarchives.org/index.php/mr/article/view/MR-045-10-1994-03_4.

Raghavan, P. 2024. Dismantling Development: Towards an Abolitionist Theory of Development. *European Journal of Development Research*, published online 16 December.

Ramirez D'Oleo, D. 2023. *This Will Not Be Generative.* Cambridge: Cambridge University Press.

Rancière, J. 1999. *Disagreement: Politics and Philosophy.* Minneapolis, MN: University of Minnesota Press.

Rancière, J. 2024. *The Politics of Aesthetics.* London: Bloomsbury Academic.

Roberts, N. 2015. *Freedom as Marronage*. Chicago: University of Chicago Press.

Robinson, C. J. 2000 [1983]. *Black Marxism: The Making of the Black Radical Tradition*. Chapel Hill, NC: University of North Carolina Press.

Robinson, C. J. 2019 [2001]. *An Anthropology of Marxism*. London: Pluto Press.

Robinson, W. I., Rangel, S. and Watson, H. A. 2022. The Cult of Cedric Robinson's Black Marxism: A Proletarian Critique. *The Philosophical Salon*, 3 October. https://thephilosophicalsalon.com/the-cult-of-cedric-robinsons-black-marxism-a-proletarian-critique/. Accessed 1 October 2024.

Rockhill, G. 2024. Editor's Introduction. In J. Rancière, *The Politics of Aesthetics*. London: Bloomsbury Academic, xiv–xix.

Rorty, R. 1999. *Philosophy and Social Hope*. London: Penguin Books.

Roy, D. 2018. *Molecular Feminisms: Biology, Becomings, and Life in the Lab*. Seattle, WA: University of Washington Press.

Samman, A. 2023. Introduction: The Desire Called Libidinal Economy. In A. Samman and E. Gammon (eds) *Clickbait Capitalism: Economies of Desire in the Twenty-First Century*. Manchester: Manchester University Press, 1–20.

Santos, B. S. 2014. *Epistemologies of the South: Justice Against Epistemicide*. Abingdon: Routledge.

Sartori, A. 2014. *Liberalism in Empire: An Alternative History*. Oakland, CA: University of California Press.

Schmidt, J. 2013. Poetry After Auschwitz – What Adorno Didn't Say. *Persistent Enlightenment*, 21 May. https://persistentenlightenment.com/2013/05/21/poetry-after-auschwitz-what-adorno-didnt-say/.

Schomerus, M. 2023. *Lives Amid Violence: Transforming Development in the Wake of Conflict*. London: Bloomsbury Academic.

Schoolman, M. 1976. Marcuse's Aesthetics and the Displacement of Critical Theory. *New German Critique* 8: 54–79.

Scott, D. 2013. On the Very Idea of a Black Radical Tradition. *Small Axe* 17(1 (40)): 1–6.

Scranton, R. 2015. *Learning to Die in the Anthropocene: Reflections on the End of a Civilization*. San Francisco, CA: City Lights.

Sen, A. 1999. *Development as Freedom*. Oxford: Oxford University Press.

Serres, M. 1995. *The Natural Contract*. Ann Arbor, MI: University of Michigan Press.

Shepherd, L. J. 2017. Aesthetics, Ethics, and Visual Research in the Digital Age: 'Undone in the Face of the Otter. *Millennium: Journal of International Studies* 45(2): 214–222.

Shotwell, A. 2016. *Against Purity: Living Ethically in Compromised Times*. Minneapolis, MN: University of Minnesota Press.

Silva, D. F. 2007. *Towards a Global Idea of Race*. Minneapolis: University of Minnesota Press.

Simpson, L. B. 2017. *As We Have Always Done: Indigenous Freedom Through Radical Resistance*. Minneapolis: University of Minnesota Press.

Smilges, J. L. 2023. *Crip Negativity*. Minneapolis, MN: University of Minnesota Press.

Snow, N. E. ed. 2024a. *The Virtue of Hope*. Oxford: Oxford University Press.

Snow, N. E. 2024b. Introduction. In N. E. Snow (ed.) *The Virtue of Hope*. Oxford: Oxford University Press, 1–45.

Sojoyner, D. M. 2017. Dissonance in Time: (Un)Making and (Re) Mapping of Blackness. In G. T. Johnson and A. Lubin (eds) *Futures of Black Radicalism*. London: Verso, 59–71.

Solnit, R. 2016. *Hope in the Dark: Untold Histories, Wild Possibilities*. Edinburgh: Canongate Books.

Spivak, G. C. 1994. Can the Subaltern Speak? In P. Williams and L. Chrisman (eds) *Colonial Discourse and Post-Colonial Theory: A Reader*. New York: Columbia University Press, 66–111.

Spivak, G. C. 2022. The Next Steps: A Preface. In M. Banerjee and J. J. P. Wouters, *Subaltern Studies 2.0*. Chicago, IL: Prickly Paradigm Press, 159–168.

Steinbock, E., Leven, B. and Valck, M. eds. 2020. *Art and Activism in the Age of Systemic Crisis: Aesthetic Resilience*. New York: Routledge.

Stockdale, K. 2021. *Hope Under Oppression*. Oxford: Oxford University Press.

Susa, R. 2019. Struggling With the Recurring Reduction of Being to Knowing: Placing Thin Hope in Aesthetic Interventions. *European Journal for Research on the Education and Learning of Adults* 10(2S): 185–199.

Swenson-Lengyel, W. 2024. Created and Fallen Hope: Theological Anthropology and Human Hoping. In N. E. Snow (ed.) *The Virtue of Hope*. Oxford: Oxford University Press, 163–199.

Terada, R. 2023. *Metaracial: Hegel, Antiblackness, and Political Identity*. Chicago, IL: Chicago University Press.

Thompson, A. 2024. Adapting Environmental Hope. In N. E. Snow (ed.) *The Virtue of Hope*. Oxford: Oxford University Press, 311–342.

Thompson, P. 2013. Religion, Utopia and the Metaphysics of Contingency. In P. Thompson and S. Žižek (eds) *The Privatization of Hope: Ernst Bloch and the Future of Utopia*. Durham, NC: Duke University Press, 82–105.

Thompson, P. and Žižek, S. eds. 2013. *The Privatization of Hope: Ernst Bloch and the Future of Utopia*. Durham, NC: Duke University Press.

Todd, S. 2015. Creating Transformative Spaces in Education: Facing Humanity, Facing Violence. *Philosophical Inquiry in Education* 23(1): 53–61.

Umezurike, G. U. 2021. The Intersection of Existential Phenomenology and Decolonial Transculturality. In C. R. Nwoma, D. Yerima-Avazi and O. Odoh (eds) *Coloniality of Knowledge in Africa: Essays in Honour of Professor Damian Opata*. Enugu, Nigeria: Abic Books & Equip, 171–196.

Van Broekhoven, L. 2020. Radical Hope as a Concept. *Pitt Rivers Museum*. https://prm.web.ox.ac.uk/radical-hope-as-a-concept. Accessed 29 September 2024.

Van der Lugt, M. 2025. *Hopeful Pessimism*. Princeton, NJ: Princeton University Press.

van Dooren, T. 2022. Animal Lessons. In M. Banerjee and J. J. P. Wouters, *Subaltern Studies 2.0*. Chicago, IL: Prickly Paradigm Press, 181–189.

Vidal, F. and Schröter, W. 2013. Can We Hope to Walk Tall in a Computerized World of Work? In P. Thompson and S. Žižek (eds), *The Privatization of Hope: Ernst Bloch and the Future of Utopia*. Durham, NC: Duke University Press, 288–299.

Viveiros de Castro, E. 2014. *Cannibal Metaphysics: For a Post-Structural Anthropology*. Minneapolis, MN: University of Minnesota Press.

Wagner, N. and Hornidge, A.-K. 2025. Unlearning Modernity? A Critical Examination of the Intergovernmental Panel on Climate Change (IPCC). *Climate Change* 178 article no. 32.

Waldow, V., Bargués, P. and Chandler, D. 2024. *Hope in the Anthropocene: Agency, Governance and Negation.* Edinburgh: Edinburgh University Press.

Warren, C. 2014. Onticide: Afropessimism, Queer Theory, and Ethics. *Ill Will*, 18 November.

Warren, C. 2015. Black Nihilism & the Politics of Hope. *Ill Will*, June.

Webb, D. 2024. Hope and the Utopian Impulse. In N. E. Snow (ed.) *The Virtue of Hope.* Oxford: Oxford University Press, 277–310.

Weiner, N. 1973. *The Human Use of Human Beings.* New York: Avon Books.

Wilderson, F. B. III 2020. *Afropessimism.* New York: W. W. Norton & Co.

Winters, J. 2016. *Hope Draped in Black: Race, Melancholy, and the Agony of Progress.* Durham, NC: Duke University Press.

Wynter, S. no date. *Black Metamorphosis: New Natives in a New World.* Institute of the Black World Records, MG 502, Box 1, Schomburg Center for Research in Black Culture.

Wynter, S. 2003. Unsettling the Coloniality of Being/Power/Truth/Freedom: Towards the Human, After Man, Its Overrepresentation–An Argument. *CR: The New Centennial Review* 3(3): 257–337.

Wynter, S. and Scott, D. 2000. The Re-Enchantment of Humanism: An Interview With Sylvia Wynter. *Small Axe* 8(1): 119–207.

Yountae, A. 2017. *The Decolonial Abyss: Mysticism and Cosmopolitics from the Ruins.* New York: Fordham University Press.

Žižek, S. 1993. *Tarrying With the Negative.* Durham, NC: Duke University Press.

Žižek, S. 2008 [1989]. *The Sublime Object of Ideology.* London: Verso.

Žižek, S. 2018. *The Courage of Hopelessness: Chronicles of a Year of Acting Dangerously.* London: Penguin Books.

INDEX

For Product Safety Concerns and Information please contact our EU
representative GPSR@taylorandfrancis.com
Taylor & Francis Verlag GmbH, Kaufingerstraße 24, 80331 München, Germany

www.ingramcontent.com/pod-product-compliance
Lightning Source LLC
LaVergne TN
LVHW061723260926
848956LV00030B/256
9781041058656